AS IT WERE

Stories of Old Columbus
VOLUME 2

Ed Lentz

RED MOUNTAIN PRESS

AS IT WERE

TO STEPHANIE

BEST REGARDS!

Ed [signature]

12/01

for Temple and Wheeler

~Contents~

Statue of Christopher Columbus on Statehouse grounds.
Photo courtesy of Ed Lentz.

~Introduction~
Some Thoughts about History in General and Local History in Particular

In the early summer of 2001, I began to think about what to say as an introduction to a second book of stories about old Columbus. And frankly, nothing much came to mind.

I am writing now after September 11, 2001—a date seared in the souls of all of us who lived through it. And it has become clearer to me what needs to be said. In a time when the world somehow seems different than it was only a few days ago, it is useful to consider both the jarring challenge of change and the consolations of continuity. It is important to reflect, that is, on the pertinence of the past.

First off, the past is not a place or a person from long ago or even the book that talks about them. The past is not even what happened back then. The past in its essence is an idea.

For thousands of years, there was no history as we understand it today. Time worked differently for our ancestors, and still does in societies more linked to the land and its cycles than our thoroughly "modern" urban society.

Should it surprise us that time itself is not an absolute thing? Not really. We like to think that some things that the human mind conceives are absolute and unchangeable—like time and space and the energy that links them. Actually we have known for most of this century that such is not the case—that permanence is an illusion and time itself a rather compressible or expandable commodity.

For much of the human past that we know of, the past served as a tool of the powerful. Tales of heroes and occasional heroines reinforced prevailing views of culture, society, law, and the traditional order of things. Some would say history still does that.

In the modern period since the Renaissance, it became increasingly fashionable to shatter the shibboleths of previous belief and argue that something called "the real past" could be found. A whole school of German scholarship argued that history should be told '*als ist eigentlich gewesen*' or 'as it actually was.' It was an appealing idea. Avoid the rhetoric of politics, social caste and religious doctrine and present the   evidence. "Just the facts, ma'am!" Some would say history still does that.

In this century we have largely rejected the idea that evidence should only serve the needs of the powerful and that evidence can be presented without bias. Today we try to tell the story several different ways and try to make our biases known. We also present a ton of evidence. Like many of the traditional disciplines, history has become a profession. Under increasing pressure to publish or perish, historians have published with a vengeance. Some of this avalanche of data is useful, interesting, and illuminating. A lot of it isn't.

Should it surprise us that if we study the contents of trash heaps, much of what we will find is trash? Should it surprise us that if we throw tons of data into a computing machine of limited creative intelligence, we will get answers of little creativity or intelligence? And should it really surprise us that if we make the presentation of our evidence dull, dreary and tedious, that people will get bored and ignore us?

What many of the people doing history forget is that most of the word 'history' is the word 'story.' We are, if we are doing our job properly, good story tellers. We should tell accurate stories, well-researched stories, honest stories—but stories all the same.

Good history is a good story. It has a beginning, a middle, and an end. And it makes a point. And that point is

usually a moral point. In short, in history as in life, good and evil exist. Right and wrong exist.

Many of our brightest people have spent much of this century telling us that since time, space, and even the deepest secrets of mind and heart are all relative—so too then truth, honor, decency, and morality must be relative too.

But most of us resist those notions. Religion continues to be popular. Parents still struggle valiantly to teach some sort of values to their children. And families not only endure, they usually prevail. Love does continue to win more often than not.

If history has value then, and it does, it is because it reinforces those values of love, truth, honor and decency for our time. It holds up a mirror, as it were, and lets us see not only our flaws but also our better selves.

Now some would say that this is a Pollyanna view of the world. The 20th Century has been the most brutal in human history. We have killed more people more efficiently than at any time in our past. We have developed means to eliminate all life on Earth and now we are preparing to take that technology to the stars. What a frightful portent.

But this also was the century that saw the destruction of monarchical power, the liberation of colonial oppression, and the fulfillment of the democratic revolutions begun in this country 200 years ago. It saw the rise of totalitarian fascism and communism and it saw its fall. It saw, at a terrible price, the good guys win.

Does this mean that bad people and bad policy have vanished? No. Does it mean that they will never return? Of course not. Does it even mean that good will always triumph? We would like to think so. But if history does have any lesson over the past 5,000 years, it is that people are enormously resilient and remarkable in their ability to triumph over adversity.

And to the frustration of the serious minded among us—and they are legion—people often seem to find a way to share some amusement while saving themselves and their world from imminent destruction.

So what then is this thing we call history? It is the record of what happened. It is an attempt to understand why these things happened. And it is an attempt to explain what difference all of this makes—to us—today—here and now.

And I suppose that is why local history is so important to me. Someone once said that all history is local history. By that, one meant that if history does not mean something to its reader—why read it? But there is more to local history than that.

In our country, we have become an increasingly homogenized people. We now have national news, national styles in dress, cuisine and entertainment, and an increasingly national style of speaking, writing and learning. In short, we continue to try to become one people.

But we are not one people.

We never have been.

And we probably never will be.

All of us have links to the pervasive past of the place we are in time. And it is a vibrantly living past. The simple problem is that many of us have not been shown how to see it.

To explain this, let us look at architecture for a moment. Thousands of us drive past the structures of our towns, villages and cities every day. And unless a house is painted purple, we do not even notice most of them. But let's say we learn what composes the residential styles of the urban America of a century ago. It will then be virtually impossible to drive through an older neighborhood without almost involuntarily noting the Italianate, Federal, and Gothic housing in the area.

As with architecture, so too we can see the living past of the city in its streets, in its structures, and in the stories of the people who made them. And once we have seen that past, it becomes a part of us forever.

Finding those stories, understanding them, and bringing them to people is what I do.

Ed Lentz
September 21, 2001

National Road mile marker.
Photo courtesy of Ed Lentz.

~1~
Coming and Going on the National Road

It was, and in many ways still is, America's Road. Across what we today call U.S. Route 40 traveled many of the new people of a new nation searching for yet something even newer. What they sought over those endless miles and through the breathtaking gaps in the green and cloud-covered mountains varied from person to person. Some sought land for a new home. Others looked for a fresh start in a new place. Still others had no idea what they really wanted. All of them moved across the thoroughfare called the National Road and made their story part of our own.

But roads can be traveled in two directions. And the interesting thing about the National Road is that it was built as much to let people out as it was to let them come into the Ohio country.

At the conclusion of the American Revolution, the new government of the United States found itself in possession of a good portion of the North American continent. This vast expanse of land was about all the victorious Americans did possess.

The simple fact was that after eight years of conflict, the government of the new United States was virtually penniless. And an army of several thousand men who had fought and suffered from Lexington to Yorktown hadn't been paid in years. Most of these soldiers were not amused to hear that they might be paid in paper currency which was not worth the paper it was printed on.

So in lieu of hard money, the Congress paid its veterans and debtholders in the one thing it did have—land. In the years following the end of the Indian Wars in Ohio, thousands of Americans poured into the Northwest Territory and made the land their own.

These people laid out towns, cleared the forests, and began to make lives for themselves on the frontier. The fact that many of the towns were never settled, many of the farms never flourished, and many of the settlers died early from fever, did not deter other newcomers from continuing to arrive.

By 1803, Ohio had enough people to petition successfully for statehood. And with statehood came increasing agitation for the federal government to do something about the deplorable state of transportation in the new country.

The roads, when they existed at all, were awful. Zane's Trace, arguably one of the best roads in the state, was little more than a rutted wagon track in the forest. Most of the other roads in the state were slightly widened Indian trails or animal paths.

Ohio by the early 1800s was producing tons of grain and thousands of commercial animals and had no easy way to get them to market. What was needed was a National Road which would permit the goods to get out and new people to come in.

But such a road would be expensive to build and maintain. And the American government had little money. Furthermore, representatives of eastern and southern states knew that providing roads to the northwest would allow these areas to prosper and better compete against the established areas on the coast. So despite the best efforts of men like Henry Clay of Kentucky, the road languished.

Finally, in 1806, Thomas Jefferson signed a bill authorizing the construction of a National Road from Cumberland, Md., to the Mississippi River. But because of continued political wrangling, the first ten miles of the road were not completed until 1811. It took 20 more years for the road to reach Columbus, Ohio. But when it did, the town was transformed.

Columbus was a small Midwestern capital town of a few thousand people in 1833. Within a year, more than 5,000 people were living in Columbus, and it became a city. Some of this growth was due to the Ohio Canal which also served Columbus, but more people used the much less expensive National Road.

The National Road entered Columbus on Main Street from the East. Originally, the plan had been to leave town on

Main Street, as well. But High Street merchants objected vociferously and successfully. So the National Road followed Main Street to High Street. At this intersection, the great highway veered sharply to the right and followed High Street to Broad Street out of the city.

This "little jog," as it was called, brought thousands of people into the heart of Columbus. It also created some of the greatest traffic jams in the history of central Ohio.

Travel on the National Road was an adventure. The great Conestoga wagons full of freight were pulled by long teams of horses, each with a rack of four to six bells attached to its harness. The approach of these wagons through a cloud of dust, dirt, and insects was a wonder to behold. In addition to the thunder of the horses and the creak of the wagons, one heard the cacophony of bells and the crack of a twelve-foot black snake whip above the team. And presiding over this thundering apparition were some people somewhat larger than life.

Leaping from the wagons at each stop were men, and an occasional woman, who were filthy dirty and spoke in a manner to match their appearance. These frontier teamsters were people of enormous appetites and a phenomenal capacity for survival. With their fellow drivers of the Concord stagecoaches, which hauled mail and passengers across the Midwest, the wagon drivers made the National Road into the stuff of legend.

With the passage of time, much of the traffic over the National Road and the Ohio Canal began to be carried by the railroads. In the mid-20th Century, the National Road got a new lease on life when truck traffic increased. Eventually the old U.S. Route 40 was superseded by the Interstate Highway System.

Yet, if one wants to see America as it was, as it still is for many people, and as many more people wish it might be as well for them, travel the National Road through Ohio. The bells in the distance are farther away than they once were, but to those who listen they can still be heard.

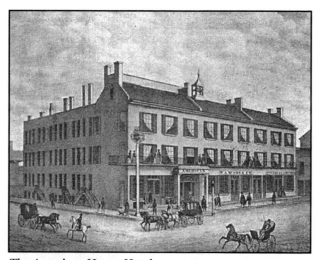

The American House Hotel.
Courtesy of the Columbus Metropolitan Library.

~2~
The American House Hotel

Columbus has always had a lot of places to stay in its downtown. In fact, in its earliest history, there wasn't much else in the downtown at all. But as trails began to be blazed through the forest and as work began on the new Statehouse, a few hardy souls began to open inns and taverns within a block or two of Statehouse Square.

These early inns left a great deal to be desired in terms of service and amenities. Usually they were two-story log houses covered with some sort of siding to protect against the weather. Inside, the ground floor was given over to the cooking and serving of food. At night, the innkeeper's family climbed a ladder to the second floor, where they slept with the guests who were not fortunate enough to find a place near the downstairs fire. All this may not have been discreet, but it certainly was cozy.

The early inns all had rather colorful names like the Swan, the Lion, the Eagle, or the Globe, and featured an elliptical sign with a picture of their namesake above the door. This was for the benefit of the great preponderance of their clientele who were not literate enough to read the name below the picture.

Local innkeepers included people like Jeremiah Robinson, who had been captured by Indians as a youth and could entertain for hours with tales of his life among them. And then there was "Squire" Shields, a self-appointed Justice of the Peace, who presided over a combination saloon and rooming house noted more for its disorder than its propriety. It went by many names, but was usually called the "War Office" for the battles which raged in the building night and day.

Most of these places were small and did not last all that long before they were replaced by larger structures or closed out by their competition. Real hotels as we understand the term today had to wait until the city was a little bigger and a little older.

The wait ended in 1835 when the Ohio Canal and the National Road arrived in Columbus and doubled the population of the city. Within a very short period of time, a number of hotels—buildings with private or semi-private rooms—began to be opened to meet the needs of a growing population.

Robert McCoy owned a dry goods store at State and High Streets and saw an opportunity. Most of the "hotels" sprouting up throughout the downtown were really adaptations of existing buildings of greater or lesser size. What was needed was a hotel that was built to be a hotel.

So McCoy tore down his building. In 1836, he erected the American House. It was an instant success. It offered nice rooms and excellent dining in an atmosphere that was positively elegant, compared to its competition.

The fact that Robert McCoy was active in local politics didn't hurt business in the hotel, either. McCoy had served on the first Columbus City Council in 1816 and would serve on every Council until he retired in the mid-1850s. His 30-year record as a councilman was something of a record. And, because of its location directly across the street from the Statehouse, the American House soon came to serve as a meeting place and home away from home for many members of the Ohio Legislature.

It was in the lobbies and rooms of the American House, and in places like the National Hotel and the Neil House a few doors away that much of the legislative business of the state and city was really decided for many years.

Through the years, the American House served its city well as a premier place for parties, receptions, and celebrations. It saw moments of hilarity such as the effort by Robert McCoy to break a ceremonial bottle of whiskey on the chimney of the newly finished hotel. To the amusement of the crowd below, McCoy broke the bottle—and then fell nearly three stories to the street before regaining his balance.

General Duncan MacArthur wasn't so lucky. The old Indian fighter had survived St. Clair's defeat, the worst beating ever given an American army by Native Americans, as well as a generation of rough and tunble state and national politics. But the American House did him in.

Walking under its long front porch one winter's day in the late 1830s, MacArthur failed to notice that the structure was creaking under the weight of snow on its roof. Without warning, the porch collapsed on MacArthur, breaking most of the major bones in his body.

With one last demonstration of what separated the frontiersman from the rest of us, MacArthur refused to die from injuries that would kill most other men instantly. Instead, he held on for three days in the very American House that had hurt him, until he finally decided to die in his own time and in his own way.

The American House had a wonderful career as a major hotel in Columbus for more than 40 years. But by the 1880s, newer and bigger buildings began to take away its trade. The owners of the building responded by turning the front part of the hotel into stores and keeping the back portion as inexpensive rental rooms. Even this compromise was not economical by the early 1920s, and most of the building was made over into retail space.

The last of the old American House was finally removed a few years ago when the Riffe State Office Tower was built on the site. As excavators cleared the corner, for a brief time the basement of the old American House appeared with its rough stone walls and the remnants of doorways leading nowhere. In a few days it was all gone, and with it went a piece of the past.

The Deardurff House, oldest house in Franklinton.
Built c. 1807.
Photo courtesy of Ed Lentz.

~3~
The Deardurff House

Approaching the front door, one can see that this house is different from a current suburban single-family home with attached garage and adjacent patio. For one thing, the walls of this house are 12 inches thick. For another, one can see that sturdy wooden shutters once could cover the few windows in this house. This was a place built with defense as well as shelter in mind. Underneath its plain frame exterior is a two-story log house. The logs are black walnut and were cut nearby when most of the area was still covered with forest. The frame exterior is also quite old, and was added at an early date to provide added protection.

The Deardurff house is still in private hands and is well locked to prevent entry by casual visitors. But a few years ago, I toured the house with the permission of its owner. The original plaster, reinforced with horsehair, is still in place; through an occasional gap one can see the foot-thick logs and the chinking between them.

In the rear of the house, the floor of the kitchen has given way, revealing a stone-lined fruit cellar beneath. But the most interesting place is the front room. The foot-wide ash and oak floor boards are scarred with the marks of literally hundreds of feet. A staircase to the rear of the house has treadboards an inch thinner in the middle than at the edges. This house has been visited by many people over many years.

And this is not surprising since the house is not only the oldest in the downtown, but for many years was also the first (and only) post office in the area. Its story and the story of the people who built it are the stuff of which legends are made.

Abraham Deardurff and his wife, Katherine, had emigrated from Germany to America in 1780 in the midst of the American Revolution. Settling on the frontier in central Pennsylvania, they began a family. Abraham left his family behind in 1797 and took a load of goods and his son, David, on a trading trip to the newly opened Ohio country. He ended up at the forks of the Scioto and Olentangy Rivers, where young Lucas Sullivant had just laid out the town of Franklinton.

Deardurff found a village of about 15 sick and exhausted people who were in desperate need of most of the goods in his pack. What he did not leave with the townsfolk, he traded with nearby Native American villages. He liked the location. So, with the proceeds of his trading, he acquired ten acres near the river close by the new town.

Clearing some trees, he and David planted a corn crop. Leaving David to clear more ground and harvest the corn, Abraham Deardurff returned to Pennsylvania for his family. The boy Abraham left behind was 14 years old, "but was big for his age."

The Deardurffs arrived back in Franklinton almost a year later on Oct. 3, 1798. Abraham brought his wife and five other children, a wagon and ox team, a milk cow, and the family's pet bulldog. In the wagon were several large wooden chests with all of the family's possessions. Among the more mundane tools, dishes, and clothing were the family's two prized possessions: a china tea set and the family Bible—printed in German. Soon the family was ensconced in a comfortable log cabin and making its way in the frontier community.

Abraham continued his trading visits to the east, carrying mail each way as well as goods for trade. To make ends meet, the family did a number of things, including operating a toll gate on the west bank of the Scioto at the river's main fording place. The family did relatively well, despite occasional visits from Indians looking for trade or company.

Though these Indians were generally friendly, they never ceased to frighten Katherine Deardurff. Leaving trade talk to her children, she would bolt the door and read her Bible until they left.

All of this changed in 1815.

In the Spring of that year, Abraham started east again for another trade trip, carrying a large sum of money. He was never seen again. His horse was found near the Virginia border with its saddle covered in blood and the moneybags emptied. It was later learned that two traders had found him stabbed and slain in the forest and had buried him where he fell.

Katherine Deardurff continued to live in Franklinton with her family until she was quite elderly. David Deardurff had built his own house in 1807. It was not a special house by any means and was similar to others like it in the growing village. It was built for protection since Franklinton was still on the frontier, and the threat of Indian attack would not end for another ten years. The house had wonderful hand-carved mantels and woodwork. But this was not because David Deardurff was wealthy—it was simply because he was a good carpenter.

For many years after it was built, the Deardurff House served as the post office for the community, with the mail arriving once a week from Chillicothe. David Deardurff lived in the house, outlived two wives, married a third, and was carried to the cemetery after a funeral in the house's parlor.

The house stayed in the family for many years, and until recently, was used as a rental apartment. There are still Deardurff descendants living in the area. But there is only one Deardurff House. It is a visible, tangible link to our past. Some local historians and neighborhood residents would like to see it saved. So should we all.

The rail crossing at High Street c. 1888.
Just north of what was once the North Graveyard.
Courtesy of the Columbus Metropolitan Library.

~4~
The North Graveyard

Columbus has had cemeteries of one sort or another for most of its history. The frontier settlement of Franklinton on the west side of the Scioto quickly created a "burying ground" on the lot surrounding its first church. The church itself was a simple log structure, but was not destined to last very long.

During the War of 1812, the building was used to store excess grain for the use of General William Henry Harrison's army. After a few months, the leaking roof of the building caused the grain to expand in volume, making the building literally burst at the seams. The cemetery remained and was used for many years. And despite the moving of many people to new cemeteries, a number of persons are still buried there.

When Columbus was founded in 1812, it was the result of a spirited contest among several central Ohio towns and villages. The winning proposal was put forth by a syndicate of four men who later styled themselves the "proprietors of Columbus." Two of the men, James McLaughlin and John Johnston, lost heavily in the economic depression of the 1820s, left Columbus, and never returned.

One of the others, Lyne Starling, was the brother-in-law of the pioneer founder of Franklinton. Something of a dandy, Starling was a lifelong bachelor who left most of his estate to found Starling Medical College, a forerunner of the OSU College of Medicine.

The last of the four proprietors was John Kerr. Kerr was Irish by lineage and a developer by disposition. It was he who introduced the partners of the original syndicate to one another. Together they bought the land constituting what is now Columbus. And it was he who not only held the syndicate together, but the town as well, through some of the darkest days of its early years.

John Kerr offered the village of Columbus one and a quarter acres for a graveyard, with the stipulation that the land would revert to his family if it were ever used for any other purpose. The land was located along the Columbus-Worthington Road to the north of the small village.

Walking north along High Street in 1813, one would have passed a few houses before reaching the swiftly rushing stream that gave Spring Street its name. Moving up the hill from Spring Street, one would have come to the city limits at what is now Nationwide Boulevard. And just beyond the city limits to the left was the North Graveyard.

Over the next 40 years and more, the cemetery would increase in size until it took up more than ten acres—a place the size of Statehouse Square. By 1845, all the lots were sold, and the superintendent reported that the site had been enclosed by a good cedar fence in the front, a rail fence in the back, and a road, now Park Street, had been built to the middle gate.

In 1848, Green Lawn Cemetery opened and many of the people in the old North Graveyard began to be moved to that place. But new burials continued.

A few more people were buried there during the Civil War, but the site became more and more disreputable. With the closing of the cemetery in 1856, maintenance stopped as well.

The entire area became overgrown with weeds and briars. The fences fell down and a variety of animals, "wild and domestick," wandered freely through. In 1864, the trustees of Green Lawn offered to trade lots with people who owned places in the North Graveyard and to move the graves to Green Lawn.

Most of the lot owners agreed to this plan. But the son of John Kerr objected, arguing that the Kerr land should revert to the family. After a lengthy series of lawsuits, title to the land was finally vested to the City of Columbus. About half the graves were opened and moved to Green Lawn in 1869. The emptied graves were left unfilled, providing a hazard to anyone straying from the increasingly poorly marked paths.

The actual removal of the balance of the graves to Green Lawn and elsewhere took until 1881. With the disposition of well-marked and well-tended graves, the task of finding the remaining plots, unmarked and often unknown, became a random proposition at best. One of the more lurid forms of feature story in the local papers of these years deals with finding yet another grave as construction proceeded in what had been the old graveyard.

In 1872, the body of a young woman was uncovered. The gold ring on her finger looked "bright as ever, but the gems with which the jewel had been set were missing." Cyrus Sells, a penitentiary guard, was killed in 1815 by a convict named Clark. His disintered skull "revealed the fatal cuts made with the axe." In the grave of one Mrs. Cole, who had been dead 31 years, were found her gold earrings, "which were presented to surviving friends."

The final spot to be searched was the marshy ground in the northeast corner of the grounds. Few graves were found, and no one wanted the site for development, so the city reserved it for use as a public market.

North Market still stands on the spot.

Canalboat Watkins, operated out of Columbus, c. 1890.
Courtesy of the Columbus Metropolitan Library.

~5~
Canals

Since their construction in the 1820s and '30s, America has had a romantic attachment to its canals.

These marvelous artificial rivers changed the face of our landscape and accelerated the growth of both our economy and our society. Yet in our nostalgia for the canals, we often forget that their era was quite brief—less than 20 years, in most places.

We also forget that this greatest public works project of its time was bitterly opposed by many people in our country who would not benefit from it.

People in Ohio generally favored the coming of the canals. Ohio and most of the Midwest had been settled with the idea that an empire was to be had in this new land. But the dream did not work out exactly as planned. Columbus, and its predecessor settlement of Franklinton, had been settled at the forks of the Scioto and Olentangy with the notion that the river would serve as an avenue for transportation and trade. It didn't. The Scioto was too treacherous to support the kind of flatboat and steamboat traffic one found on other rivers in the state.

So for more than 20 years, the new capital of Ohio was land-locked and isolated from easy commerce with the ports to the east and the south.

By the 1820s, the clamor for "internal improvements" that would benefit the growing states in the Midwest was becoming a political rallying cry. In response to this pressure, the National Road began to move across Pennsylvania toward Ohio.

But a national road, while helpful, was not enough. More and more Ohioans looked with envy on the elaborate Erie Canal system being developed in New York and wanted something similar for themselves.

Leading the campaign was Alfred Kelley, a state legislator from Cleveland who had moved to Columbus in 1816. Kelley was thin, austere, and an easy man to dislike intensely. He was also absolutely brilliant, ferociously energetic, and consistently honest in his dealings. And it was said he drove no one as hard as he drove himself.

Kelley not only had the vision to see what a canal could do for Ohio, he also had the political savvy to bring it about. He and a small group of political and financial associates brought the canals into being. With a creative use of public financing and his own close personal supervision, Ohio's canals were largely completed by the late 1830s. But it wasn't easy.

In the late 1830s, a tide of rampant economic expansion collapsed in the "panic" or depression of 1837. Scrambling to keep itself solvent, Ohio government found itself unable to pay the interest on its canal bonds. If the bonds went into default, the canal system would collapse.

Unwilling to see the project fail, Kelley pledged his own house as collateral to save the canal system.

The Greek Revival "House that Saved Ohio" stood immediately to the east of Memorial Hall (the former site of COSI) until it was torn down in 1962 to make way for the Christopher Inn, itself torn down a number of years ago. Disassembled stone by stone, the pieces of the Kelley Mansion have had a number of homes over the years.

Ohio had two major canal systems—the Miami and Erie in the west and the Ohio and Erie in the east. The main line of the Ohio and Erie ran from Portsmouth to Cleveland and missed Columbus. Because of political as well as economic pressure, a "feeder canal" was built, linking the capital city to the canal. The feeder canal branched off near Canal Winchester and headed in a generally western direction through Lockbourne until it neared the Scioto River.

Just before it reached the river, the feeder made an

18

abrupt righthand turn and headed due north toward Columbus. It entered the city to the east of the river and emptied into the Scioto at what is now Bicentennial Park. The canal flowed along the western wall of the Cultural Arts Center. The Waterford tower is built on the old canal bed. A historical plaque marks the spot.

The canal age in Ohio ended with the coming of the railroad. Railroads were cheaper to build and maintain and could go places canals couldn't. The first railroad to enter the city, the Columbus and Xenia, was completed in 1850. By 1855, five railroads passed through Columbus, and the number of lines continued to grow until well after the Civil War.

By 1860, the canal system was formally closed by the state. Parts of the canal continued to be used for private hauling, but other sections became little more than open sewers. The great flood of 1913 obliterated major portions of the remaining sections of the waterway, and the system was largely abandoned thereafter.

But some of the lakes built to provide water to the canal during dry seasons continue to be used for pleasure and for flood control. In central Ohio, Buckeye Lake is the largest of these. Every few years, there is revived discussion of reopening abandoned sections of the canal for use, or even of building new canals. Usually these discussions do not go very far because of the immense cost of such an undertaking in an era of tight budgets and scarce resources. Or perhaps it's simply because we do not have an Alfred Kelley among us at the moment.

To get a sense of what canal life was like, visit the abandoned locks to the east of Lockbourne. Or better yet, take a ride on one of the restored sections of the canal near Piqua, Roscoe Village, or Canal Dover. It may be one of the slower rides you've taken recently, but it is also one of the quietest. And there is something to be said for quiet transportation.

Columbus Police Department of 1908.
Courtesy of the Columbus Metropolitan Library.

~6~
Keeping the Peace

There were no local police in Columbus until 1816. Columbus was born during the War of 1812, and after four years of conflict, the place was finally incorporated as a borough. The town consisted of a few public buildings on Statehouse Square, a few muddy streets, and a host of taverns, inns, and shops clustered in small, temporary buildings nearby.

Law and order was not totally lacking, since the county sheriff had been on the job for several years. And a local militia consisting of several veterans of the recent unpleasantness with Great Britian was available if things got totally out of hand. And they often did, with the help of that selfsame militia, that liked to celebrate the end of muster day in ways that gave new meaning to the term "disturbing the peace."

It did not take too long for the civic leaders of the new capital city to come up with solutions to these problems. The office of Village Marshal was created, and one Samuel King was the first to fill the post. Marshal King created a night watch which not only patrolled for malefactors, but also kept an eye out for any other situations that might deserve a fine. These included such things as letting one's pigs run free or "discharging a firearm west of Fourth Street."

Frederick Spade was the first and only member of the night watch for some time. While Spade struggled valiantly against the forces of evil, it soon became apparent that evil was winning. The ultimate answer to the problem of vice and lawlessness in Columbus in the early days was not to eliminate it, but to isolate it.

Jonesburgh was a crossroads collection of saloons, vice dens, and stolen property emporiums that stood outside the limits of town about where Cleveland Avenue intersects with the Innerbelt. The unspoken arrangement was that the worst of the population would consort and trade at that location and leave the good people of Columbus alone.

Over the next 20 years, the office of the marshal grew with the village. In 1834, because of the canal and the National Road, Columbus had reached a population of 5,000 and officially became a city. The village marshal now became an elected city marshal, and police work became politically partisan for the next several decades.

Until 1850, there was no separate jail for the city of Columbus, the county jail apparently meeting the needs of the area. But continued growth led to the inclusion of two jail cells in the city office section of the new Central Market House completed in that year near Fourth and Town Streets. Even this facility soon proved to be inadequate and a separate jail facility was built at Lazelle and Walnut Streets in 1855, with eleven cells and a meeting space.

The Civil War transformed Columbus and its public institutions, as well. In 1868, an ordinance established the size of the City Marshal's force at 25 men, and adopted a navy blue uniform for the first time. Up to this point, the officers dressed in civilian clothes and simply wore a pewter badge to identify themselves.

Between the end of the Civil War and the turn of the century, Columbus experienced enormous growth and change. The old vice district of Jonesburgh had been burned down by an irate mob, but had been replaced by new "evil vicinities," like the "Badlands" and "Rowdies Row." In most cases, these districts were located just outside the city limits and near major thoroughfares. The police did by all accounts a reasonable job of keeping the "worst of the worst" confined to these districts, while trying to keep the police force itself intact. Police work in the late 1800s was intensely political. Job security in the police department was precarious at best, since a change in politics could lead to a wholesale removal of the police force. Some of the conflicts between contending factions within the department were memorable, with one side barricading itself inside the police station, to prevent the other half from entering.

Ultimately, this politicization was resolved with the establishment of a non-political Metropolitan Police Force over a period of several years. By the turn of the century, most of the worst excesses had been eliminated, a rudimentary Civil Service system had been put in place, and a new Police Station had been built near the intersection of Town and Front Streets.

And while the Columbus Police Department changed with the times by replacing horses with motor cars and call boxes with radios, the forces they were contending with changed, as well. With all of the trials and tribulations faced by local peace officers, it is still interesting to note that the first death in the line of duty did not take place until 1899. In that year, Detective Abe Kleeman was killed in a stand-up shootout with one Charles Dumont, who also died in the battle. Kleeman's partner, George Gaston, was shot in the forehead but survived, and carried the bullet to the grave.

The old Town Street police station was severely damaged in the Great Flood of 1913, and was replaced by a new station at Gay Street and Marconi Boulevard in 1930. That facility is still standing but its future became unclear when the magnificent new Central Police Station opened in 1991.

A visit to these buildings is a great experience. The people within have some wonderful stories to tell—stories of courage, and service, and of ordinary people doing extraordinary things for all of us—every day.

The "Pride of Columbus" c.1900.
Courtesy of the Columbus Metropolitan Library.

7

Firefighting in Columbus

The surprising thing about the early history of fires in Columbus is that there were so few of them at first. In 1822, the "first fire of any consequence took place... Eight buildings were burned." Fortunately, only one of them was an occupied dwelling. And not surprisingly, Council quickly passed an ordinance to "prevent destruction by fire in the Borough of Columbus."

The ordinance provided for a hook and axe company of 15 men, a ladder company of 12 men, and one company of 12 men to protect property. All of these people were volunteers, although persons could be drafted if necessary to fill out the companies.

In addition, the Town Marshal was required to ring a bell upon hearing the first alarm of a fire. Every store, shop, or dwelling in the village was required to have readily available ten-quart buckets of "good jacked leather." And when the alarm sounded, every available able-bodied man between 15 and 50 was to assist the fire companies by forming a bucket brigade.

This system was augmented by a "fire engine" in 1823. The engine consisted of a manually operated water pump on wheels, which in short order came to be called "The Tub." In 1824, permission was gained to build an "engine house" on Statehouse Square. Really a glorified shed, the building stood just to the east of the original Statehouse at State and High, and would serve as the city's only recognized firehouse for almost 30 years.

The history of fire suppression in Columbus in the 1800s is a story of government providing resources with only the greatest reluctance and counting mostly on volunteers to do the actual firefighting. Fire prevention was always recommended but seldom implemented because a professional fire service was virtually nonexistent.

Instead, numerous volunteer fire companies sprang up around the city. Often well-equipped by private donations, these companies were impressively uniformed and in some cases were even trained to fight fires. Some men joined the fire companies because they were a wonderful mix of service group and fraternal society. Others joined as well because firefighters were exempt from jury duty and militia service. But as one volunteer wrote in the 1840s, "I went to fight fires because it was great fun most of the time."

As Columbus grew and the bucket lines from the river grew longer and longer, Council finally gave in and built a system of cisterns at each of the major intersections of High Street from Broad to Mound. Each of these cisterns held 6,000 gallons of water and would meet the initial water needs of the people fighting the fire.

Volunteer firefighters not only fought fires. They also fought each other. Since the most effective fire companies were private, building owners often had standing offers to handsomely pay the first company to arrive if the building was burning. If two companies arrived at the same time, a donnybrook often resulted, as rival companies fought each other for the honor of fighting the fire.

Sometimes, the fire companies were drafted for other purposes, as well. In the early 1840s, a rather disreputable vice den sprang up between the respectable Clinton Bank and the rather pretentious Tontine Coffee House. On one evening when the frivolities got more raucous than usual, a local fire company emptied the contents of an entire street cistern into the building to put out an alleged fire. Much to the satisfaction of its neighbors, the "notorious nest"quickly closed and never reopened.

By the 1850s, the rapid growth of Columbus had led to the construction of three more firehouses to store equipment and supplies and the purchase of several more pieces of equipment. But most of the firefighting was still being done by volunteers. The event which changed all this was—as one might expect—a spectacular fire.

On Nov. 6, 1860, the most fashionable hotel in Columbus, the original Neil House Hotel, burned to the ground. Not only was the building directly across the street from the Statehouse and adjacent to two cisterns, but the hotel even sponsored its own fire company. None of this was to any avail, however, as dry conditions, a strong wind, and lots of flammable material took their toll. Working valiantly through the night, every local fire company and most of the rest of the population of Columbus saved the rest of the block and kept the fire from spreading.

After this disaster, it was finally recognized that Columbus needed a professional fire service. Small at first, the Columbus Fire Department over the next century gradually grew in size and professional expertise. Horse-drawn steam pumpers replaced earlier, hand-operated pumps, and a "new" generation of fire stations began to be built around the city. Many of these older fire stations are still standing.

One of them, Engine House Number Five, is a restaurant, while other uses for old stations include a meeting hall and a retail store. The survival and reuse of these buildings is gratifying. But the most impressive of the older firehouses is Engine House Number One, which underwent major renovation to become a Fire Museum for the City of Columbus. Financed by private donations and the time and energy of current and former Columbus firefighters and their friends, the Museum will serve as a fitting tribute to the people who risked their lives "tasting the smoke" for the rest of us.

Double hanging at the Ohio Pen, 1844.
Drawing c. 1884.
Courtesy of the Columbus Metropolitan Library.

28

8

Public Justice

It was not the first event of its kind in the Columbus area. It would not be the last. But the public execution of William Clark and Esther Foster on Feb. 9, 1844, had a certain distinction in its own right.

Most executions at the old Ohio Penitentiary on Spring Street since 1855 and at other locations prior to that time were "public" in the sense that members of the public witnessed them. But they were generally rather low-key and subdued affairs. The public hanging of Clark and Foster was anything but that.

Part of the reason for the notoriety and prominence of this exercise in public justice was due to the nature of the crimes and the criminals. Part of it was due to the novelty of a public execution, an event not seen in Columbus all that often. And part of it was undoubtedly due to the nature of the capital city itself.

Between 1840 and 1850, Columbus grew from a population of 6,048 to more than 17,882. The number of people in Franklin County likewise increased from 24,880 to 42,909. The coming of the Ohio Canal and the National Road in the mid-1830s had seen Columbus change from a rural village into a small but thriving town. Now the town was becoming a city.

Columbus had been settled by a restless population moving west from New England and the South seeking a new life in a new country of inexpensive land and unlimited opportunity. Now political revolution and economic upheaval was causing the same kind of migration by thousands of persons from Ireland, Germany, and elsewhere in Western Europe. Many of those people ended up in the Midwest in general and in Ohio in particular.

By 1850, almost half the population of Columbus would be of recent German origin, one quarter would be Irish, and the rest would be the folks who were here before all of those Irish and Germans showed up.

Columbus, a rough-and-ready crossroads town before the migrations of the 1840s, became even rougher and readier. This change in the pace of urban life was reflected in the evolution of the Ohio penitentiary.

Originally located where the Cultural Arts Center stands today, at Main Street and Civic Center Drive, the Ohio Penitentiary was originally nothing more than a big stone house with a large back yard that moved down a slope toward the flats along Scioto Street and the river.

Overcrowded and not particularly secure, the prison was ready for a move by the 1830s, when the arrival of the Ohio Canal forced the issue. State officials decided to keep the prison near the capital city but move it "out into the country" where the air and water would be cleaner, room for expansion was available, and nearby fields could be used to grow food for the facility.

"Nearby," in this case, was along Spring Street on a ten-acre tract just outside the city limits at West Street. The prison would stay there for more than 150 years. But by the early 1840s, the original building was already outgrown. Even with the addition of more land and the construction of more buildings, the Ohio Penitentiary was a festering nest of disease, despair, and, much too often, early and untimely death.

Death sometimes came in the form of epidemic disease, as in the cholera epidemics that ravaged the prison in the 1830s and 1840s. It sometimes involved sudden conflict among the predominantly male inmate population. But sometimes violence visited others, as well. And when it did, the results were more public.

In 1843, inmate William Clark attacked prison guard Cyrus Sells with a cooper's axe and killed him with one stroke. Close by, in the separate and much smaller women's prison, inmate Esther Foster attacked another woman inmate with a fire shovel. She did not dispatch her antagonist with one blow, but with repeated effort managed to kill her opponent as well.

In the trials that followed, Clark pleaded insanity. Foster's defense was that the crime was unpremeditated and therefore not deserving of the death penalty. Neither defense prevailed.

And so it happened that on a chill day in February 1844, a double gallows came to be used in Columbus. It was built in the flats along Scioto Street, near the canal basin and the site of the old prison. Sheriff William Domigan presided and hoped for swift and efficient dispensation of justice. It was not to be.

A huge crowd turned out to witness the execution. In the words of one observer, "Many of the citizens of the town prudently refused to witness the scene." But many more people, male and female, decided to attend. It was a scene of "noise, confusion and drunkenness and disorder." In the course of events, both Clark and Foster were executed. In the excitement, a horse broke loose and ran into the crowd, injuring several people and crushing a longtime Columbus resident named Sullivan Sweet under its hooves.

It is not known where Clark and Foster were buried. It was often common practice to bury executed felons under their gallows. If that was the case, the gravesite is now underwater, since the widening of the Scioto River in this century removed that low ground. More than likely was the swift and unmarked burial of the two people in the small graveyard near the new penitentiary, where Foster's victim was probably buried, as well. Cyrus Sells, the prison guard, was buried in the Old North Graveyard. His grave was found in the 1870s when the occupants of the cemetery were removed and reburied elsewhere to make way for the North Market. William Clark achieved a certain notoriety after his death. One of the main attractions of Walcutt's Dime Museum in downtown Columbus was "a good wax figure likeness" of the axe murderer. The museum has been closed for many years and the location of its contents, including the "good wax figure" is not known. And, perhaps, that is just as well.

Dentist's office c. 1898.
Courtesy of the Columbus Metropolitan Library.

~9~

Hiram Todd and Frontier Dentistry

Today many people probably can think of things they would rather be doing than visiting the dentist. But with modern equipment, ample supplies, and a pleasant office, a trained professional can make a trip to the dentist often painless and at least minimally endurable. It was not always that way.

Hiram Todd was born in Plymouth, Connecticut in 1808. He entered the profession of dentistry after his primary education, and by 1825 had established a practice in New York City. By 1830, he had decided that his future lay elsewhere. He came to Columbus and took up residence at 160-1/2 South High Street. Today that is in the heart of the downtown central business district. In those days, High Street south of Town Street was predominantly residential.

At that time Columbus had a population of only a few thousand people. For a few months of every year when the legislature and courts were in session, the town was a busy place. But for the rest of the year, it was a quiet Midwestern town. Hiram Todd soon discovered that it was difficult to make a living as a dentist in Columbus.

Dr. Lincoln Goodale had had the same problem trying to make ends meet as a practicing physician. People had little money for doctors and even less trust in their methods. Rather than attempting to continue his work while he waited for the town to grow, Dr. Goodale gave up medicine and went into the retail business. He opened what would later be called a general store and within a few years had made a fortune. Goodale Park is the gift of the good doctor to the city where he had prospered.

Unlike Dr. Goodale, Dr. Todd was committed to his profession. Unable to make ends meet by staying in one place, Dr.

Todd took his practice on the road. Basing himself out of Columbus, he traveled the back roads of central Ohio, bringing his dental expertise to the people who needed it. A lot of people needed it.

In the mid-1800s, most people were not as aware of the principles of dental hygiene as the average eight-year-old of our own era. If one eats a lot of different things without brushing one's teeth from time to time, one will eventually develop dental problems. Of course there were mitigating circumstances. Since much of the water in the small towns had become polluted by placing wells and privies in close proximity, many people consumed a daily ration of alcohol. And while the alcohol caused a host of problems of its own, at least it had the benefit of disinfecting the mouth from time to time.

Also, many people simply could not afford to eat much more than they could grow, shoot or catch. This meant that sugar, the grand poobah of tooth decay, was a luxury and not consumed as often as it is today. This meant that many of the people Hiram Todd was called upon to treat were folks who were a little better off than their friends and who, suffering from their success, could also afford to pay him with something resembling money.

Coming into a small town, like most of the dentists of his time, Todd would treat people in their homes. An ideal way to do this was to place the patient in a rocking chair and when the right angle was reached, to place a log under the rockers. In this position the patient could be ministered to in a convenient if not painless manner.

Then as now, a tooth could either be saved or it couldn't. If it could be saved, the practitioner used a small hand powered drill to remove the offending decay. As might be imagined, this took a while. Eventually, amalgams of gold or silver would be used to fill cavities. But in the early days a variety of other soft metals including lead were used. The result was a filling that caused lead poisoning.

If the offending tooth could not be saved it had to be removed. To do this the dentist had several tools at his disposal. The forceps, basically a pair of pliers, was tried. If this didn't work well, a wicked-looking device called a pelican was employed. Essentially a pair of pliers with one flat side and one curved side, the pelican allowed the dentist to gain angled leverage. Finally there was a device called the key, which resembled a modern basin wrench. With this device the practitioner twisted the tooth out of its socket, occasionally taking an adjacent tooth with it. All of this was done without anesthesia. It was not a pretty sight.

Apparently, Dr. Todd was better than most at this painful business because he made a success of himself as an itinerant dentist. Returning to Columbus in the wake of its rapid growth because of the arrival of the Ohio Canal and National Road, Dr. Todd established himself as the city's first resident dentist.

Todd met his future wife while on the road in Granville in 1831. The Todds raised two daughters and a son while Dr. Todd built his dental practice. William Todd followed his father into dentistry and for more than 70 years the Todd family cared for the dental needs of Columbus.

Over those years, dentistry changed quite a bit. The introduction of anesthesia, power dental equipment, and effective supplies and medicines complemented the emergence of dentistry as a profession requiring extensive education, training and licensing. By the time Hiram died in 1884 he had lived to see much of this transformation.

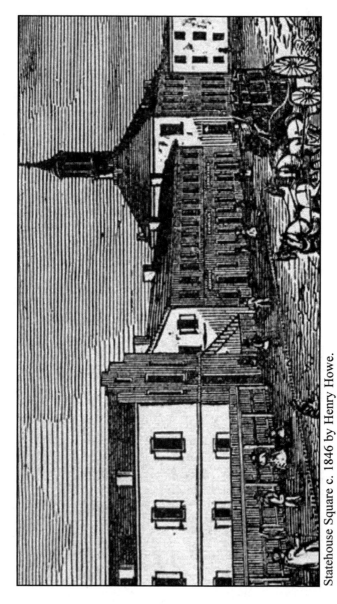

Statehouse Square c. 1846 by Henry Howe.
From *Historical Collections of Ohio*, Derby and Broadway, 1847.
Courtesy of the Columbus Metropolitan Library.

~10~
The Night the Statehouse Burned

To this day, the exact reasons for the destruction of Ohio's Statehouse in a late-night winter fire in 1852 are still unclear. But this much is certain: the fire destroyed the building that was the reason for the existence of the capital city. And the fire was set.

The first capital was established in Chillicothe in 1803, and the General Assembly held forth from there for a few years. But in relatively short order, the residents of the rest of the state in general, and northern Ohio in particular, began to complain that a more central location was needed. For two years, the legislature tried to oblige by shifting the capital to Zanesville, but eventually it moved back to Chillicothe. Much of the reason for the Chillicothe location was convenience. Most of the state had been settled from the south along the Ohio River corridor. Many of the gentlemen of property and standing who formed the leadership of early Ohio lived nearby.

But by 1810, the pressure had become politically unbearable. So, as legislatures are wont to do when faced with tasks they really don't want to do, the Ohio General Assembly appointed a committee to find a new home for the state capital.

And so Columbus was born on Feb. 14, 1812.

Work on the new capital proceeded very slowly because of the War of 1812. It was not until 1816 that the legislature finally met for the first time in Columbus. The town itself was a modest collection of frame and log structures housing about 600-700 people. Another several hundred people lived across the river in the older and considerably more well-developed frontier community of Franklinton.

A ten-acre lot had been cleared and was called Statehouse Square, but dead trees and brush still littered the grounds and provided shelter to animals from the nearby forest, as well as several dozen local pigs.

And in the midst of these rustic homes and stores—and more than a few inns and taverns—were three buildings that immediately caught one's attention. Standing at Broad and High, one immediately saw the two-story stone courthouse with its distinctive and rather garish bright green tower. Next to it, to the south along the east side of High Street, stood the simple two-story brick building used as state offices. And finally, at the northeast corner of State and High Streets, stood the Statehouse.

It was a relatively simple two-story brick building capped by a wooden bell tower. Intentionally simple in design, it was nevertheless a cut above the other buildings in town. Most of the other homes and businesses in town had few, if any, windows. The Statehouse had a lot of them. Most places had crude floors, if any at all. The Statehouse had solid walnut waxed and oiled floors and more than a little carved wooden trim on oak, maple, cherry, and walnut. The furnishings were simple, as well, but were also sturdy and well made. And in the cupola above the building was a bell—one of the few in the entire state.

For the next 35 years, the Ohio General Assembly met in this building, the House of Representatives on the ground floor and the Senate on the floor above. For the first decade or so, the modest building served the needs of the new state quite well. But just as the state grew apace with the arrival of canals, roads, and railroads, so too did the needs—real and presumptive—of the legislature.

By 1838, ground had been broken for a large, new, and quite elegant Statehouse. It was assumed that the new building would take two years to construct and cost about $200,000.

By 1850, after more than a dozen years, the building was still not done. Political bickering, construction problems, and just plain bad luck had plagued the project for most of its life. Both legislators and residents began to talk openly of trying to find a way to speed things along.

On the evening of Feb. 1, 1852, a person or persons unknown did just that. It was a Sunday evening in the dead of winter. At four o'clock in the morning, the cry of "Fire!" rang through the town when it was learned that a fire was burning in the middle of the floor of the upstairs Senate chamber in the Statehouse.

That fire was almost extinguished when it was discovered that the timbers overhead were on fire, as well. After an unsuccessful attempt to fight the flames, bystanders watched the belfry collapse on to the Senate floor, followed by the roof of the building. Soon, the entire building was engulfed in flame.

For the next five years, the legislature met in various public meeting halls until the new Statehouse was finally finished enough to be occupied. Interestingly, despite the lateness of the hour and the inclemency of the weather, volunteers managed to save most of the furniture, books, and papers of the House of Representatives. The journals of the Clerk of the Senate were saved, as well. And no serious effort was ever made to determine how the fire had come to break out in the middle of the open floor of the Senate chamber.

It may say something for the feelings of many at the loss of the old building that the cracked bell from the Statehouse belfry was melted down and a number of miniature bells were cast from the metal. They were said to have sold briskly and well.

Today, Ohio's Statehouse—the new one that took 22 years to build—has been wonderfully restored and is worth a visit. If you go, visit the exhibits on the lower level that show the history of the building through the years. Somewhat removed from the rest and near the northwest light well is a small bell—a souvenir from the night the Statehouse burned.

The Columbus YMCA.
Photo courtesy of Ed Lentz.

~11~
The YMCA

According to its founding legend, the Young Men's Christian Association got its start not among the deperately poor of the crowded cities, nor even among the rakes and reprobates of the privileged and proper classes. Rather, this great and good organization got its start because of Depravity among the Drygoods.

A group of twelve retail store clerks gathered together for the first time at the home of one George Williams in London, England, on the evening of June 6, 1844. Williams, a young shop clerk, was appalled by the conditions facing young men who came to the city to find their fortunes. Surely, he wrote, "there was no class more degraded and dissolute, none of whom were sunk deeper in ungodliness and dissipation, than the shopmen of London." Since Mr. Williams was a clerk himself, he presumably knew whereof he spoke.

The group of similarly outraged young men formed a society whose purpose was the "improvement of the spiritual condition of young men, by the introduction of religious services among them."

A number of groups like this came and went over the years as people of good will tried to cope with the terrors and temptations of urban life. But the YMCA endured.

And since England did not have a monopoly on rapidly growing and deeply troubled cities in the mid-1800s, it was not too long before the idea spread to other countries as well.

In 1855, the YMCA came to Columbus. As it turned out, it was a very good year for a group dedicated to the uplifting of young men to arrive in the rapidly growing city.

Columbus had been little more than a sleepy Midwestern capital until the mid-1830s. Over the following 20 years, the town's population doubled, and then doubled again, until there were more than 15,000 people living in a town that had originally been designed for about 2,000 souls.

People were crammed into very tight quarters. The city was frigid in the winter and a furnace in the summer. And through it all, there were virtually no working sanitary sewers. Disease was rampant and many people drowned their worries in drink. It was an explosive mixture.

To say that the newcomers, mostly immigrants, did not get along with one another would be an understatement. On July 4, 1855, a German parade was attacked by bystanders. The parade participants were armed to the teeth and a full-scale battle erupted at the corner of Town and High Streets. The truly remarkable thing was that only one person was killed in the ensuing melee.

It was into this rather turbulent world that the YMCA was born in Columbus at a meeting of 40 men on Jan. 15, 1855, at the Old First Presbyterian Church (where the Hyatt on Capitol Square stands today). The leader of the group was Henry B. Carrington, a young attorney and son-in-law of Lucas Sullivant, one of the area's pioneer settlers.

Carrington went on to serve in the Civil War and as a military commander in the opening of the far West. He achieved some notoriety in his later career as the commander of one Captain Fetterman, who claimed to one and all that, with 80 men, he could ride through the whole Sioux Nation. Unfortunately, Fetterman tried to prove it, and his force was wiped out to the last man.

The YMCA languished during the Civil War, simply because most of the young men it served were away. But the group received a new lease on life in the late 19th century, as urban conditions seemed to get worse rather than better.

And while many similar groups came and went over the years, the YMCA grew and thrived. The reasons for its success were many. The group skillfully blended its message of moral uplifting with a practical program of physical training and educational classes. More importantly, the YMCA became well-known for being able to provide young men with inexpensive, safe, and healthful lodging and meals.

The "Y" has had several homes in Columbus over the years. But by 1892, the group had relocated to a five-story structure on Capitol Square. It seemed at the time that the building would be large enough to last the group forever.

Forever in this case was the 18 years it took the group to grow from 617 to 1,682 members. In 1916, a new site was purchased at the corner of Spring and Front Streets. By 1924, a new building was completed at the then extraordinary cost of $1.45 million. At the time it opened, it was the largest YMCA in the world.

Over the years, the YMCA in Columbus has pioneered a number of innovative programs for the community. What is now Franklin University got its start at the YMCA, as did the institution that ultimately became the Capital University Law School. More importantly, over the past 75 years, more than 9.4 million people have resided in the building. And as one might imagine, over 9 million people do cause just a bit of wear and tear. The YMCA recently completed a total renovation the historic structure. It was not only a good investment in the future of Columbus, but a thrifty one, as well. It would have cost more than $60 million to construct a new building with similar facilities.

The YMCA has been a positive force in the city of Columbus for almost seven generations. And once again the Y is in the position to begin to help for seven more. There are few organizations in Columbus with such a legacy of service. It is well deserving of our support.

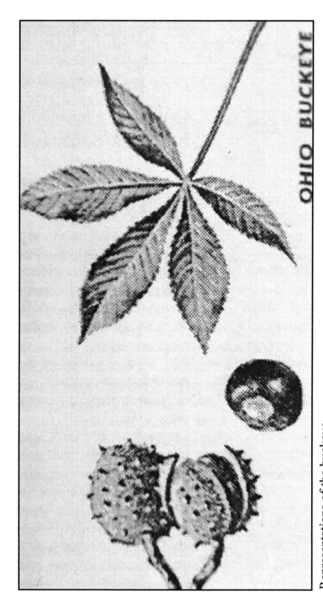

Representations of the buckeye.
Photo courtesy of Ed Lentz.

44

The Buckeye State

Ohio is the Buckeye State. The Ohio State University's athletic teams are all called 'Buckeyes'. And there are enough companies, organizations, and associations with 'Buckeye' in their names to fill a modest telephone directory of their own. So how did this all come to be and what exactly is a buckeye, anyway?

First and foremost, a buckeye is NOT the eyeball of a deer. It just looks like the eyeball of a deer. Which is why the Indians called the fruit of a variant of the horse chestnut family 'hetuck' or, as we have translated it, 'buckeye'.

Ohio, in the frontier period, had a lot of buckeye trees. They grew quickly and were quite large in comparison with many other trees in the unbroken forests of those days. In fact, one of the earliest references to a person as a buckeye is a Native American compliment to one of the original settlers of Marietta, calling him a 'big buckeye'. This is probably a reference to the tree rather than the small brown sphere with a big white spot.

But this is not why the people of Ohio are called 'Buckeyes'. To understand how we all came to be named after a tree, we must first look at medicine and then, of all things, at politics.

Medicine on the frontier was something fundamentally different than medicine as we understand it today. Instead of trusting in the skills of the physicians of the period (assuming you could find one), many people relied on a mixture of home remedies, bed rest, healthy food, and a little prayer to get them by. And some of the home remedies people relied on used the leaves, bark, and fruit of the buckeye tree. In fact, the buckeye tree seems in its own way to have been something of a one-stop drugstore.

A tea made from the tree seems to have been used extensively as a treatment for malaria. This must have been a tricky medicine to make since much of bark and covering of the buckeye itself contains a deadly poison. So this is not something one would want to try at home without some guidance.

Over the years, the buckeye has been used to treat a variety of ailments including varicose veins, respiratory infections, and severe diarrhea. It has also been used externally to treat cuts and bruises, frostbite, ringworm, and hemorrhoids. How it was used in all of these cases is not fully clear from the sources, and I am not really sure I want to know.

In any case, the buckeye was well-established as both a medicinal aid and a prominent part of the landscape in the early days of the settlement of Ohio.

And this brings us to how Columbus figured in the making of Ohio as the Buckeye State.

In 1840, William Henry Harrison ran for President on the Whig Party ticket. While the Whigs were relatively new on the national political scene, Harrison himself was enormously popular. Beginning his career as a young aide to Anthony Wayne at the Battle of Fallen Timbers, Harrison had gone on to win an important victory at Tippecanoe in 1811, and mobilized the American armies who finally won several spectacular victories in the War of 1812 in the west. He later had served in several important political posts.

He was well known throughout the area then known as 'the West' and that we today call the Midwest.

In attempting to belittle his candidacy, an opposition newspaper claimed that Harrison "was better fitted to sit in a log cabin and drink hard cider than rule in the White House." This was an ironic comment to make about a man who had a handsome home on the Ohio River and probably had not seen the inside of a log cabin in many years. But the Whig Party seized on this common man imagery of Harrison and made it their own. In town after town in 1840, political rallies were held with a wagon carrying a small log cabin festooned with strings of buckeyes and raccoon skins drying on their outside walls.

One of the biggest rallies occurred in Columbus at the end of February, 1840, and the contingent from Clark County came to town with their own cabin on a wagon. Entering Columbus, they sang this song:

Oh where, tell me where
was your buckeye cabin made
Twas built among the merry boys
who wield the plow and spade
Where the log cabins stand
in the bonnie buckeye shade.

Oh what, tell me what
is to be your cabin's fate
We'll wheel it to the capital and place it there elate
for a token and a sign of the bonnie buckeye state.

The buckeye became a symbol of the Whig Party in the west and of its candidate William Henry Harrison, who eventually won the Presidency in the fall of 1840.

From that point on, the term 'buckeye' came to be accepted as a term for an Ohioan. In the mid-1840s, a journalist named S.S. Cox went abroad and wrote a series of articles from Europe signed 'A Buckeye Abroad.' His readers in Ohio and across the country knew exactly where he was from. We still do.

The Kelton House, reported to have been a "stop" on the "Underground Railroad," as it stands today.
Photo courtesy of Ed Lentz.

~13~
The Finney "Kidnapping"

Ohio in the late 1840s was a cauldron that was slowly but surely being brought to a boil. The clash of cultures of Yankee versus Southerner, which had dominated the early politics of the state, was being ethnically transformed by the arrival of German, Irish, and other immigrants. And to this heady brew were added new and dangerous conflicts over what President Lincoln came to call "The Peculiar Institution"—chattel slavery in a land pledged to freedom. As the state capital, Columbus, of course, was figuratively and literally in the middle of all of this.

At the end of the American Revolution, the new government of the United States had found itself with little money, a lot of land, and a large number of unpaid soldiers. The obvious answer was to pay the army in land. A huge, pie-shaped wedge of land from the Miami River to the Scioto was set aside for Virginia veterans. Another large chunk of real estate in northeast Ohio was reserved for Connecticut soldiers.

By 1803, when Ohio became a state, some of the results of all this was a settlement of Virginians at the forks of the Scioto and Olentangy, called Franklinton. It was one of the most northern of the "southern" settlements in the state at that time. Complementing it were places like Worthington to the north, which had been settled by Connecticut residents.

Slavery had never really been much of an issue to people coming to Ohio. The Northwest Ordinance of 1787 had forever banned slavery in the new territories north of the Ohio River. Of course many southerners brought their slaves to Ohio, freed them, and then kept these people in their "employ" for a period of time. And many white Ohioans looked with disdain on black people, whether they were literally or only nominally "free."

But many did not. Ohio was an early center of anti-slavery activity and by the 1830s was rivaling Massachusetts and Pennsylvania as a hotbed of opposition to slavery in any and all of its forms. Many of the future leaders of Ohio and the nation got their practical education in the volatile politics of 1840s Ohio, where a rising tide of opposition to slavery was being met by increasing defiance by the South to northern "meddling" in southern life.

And part of that education included the case of an unfortunate man named Jerry Finney. Finney was a black man who had come to Columbus in the 1830s when the frontier village was quickly becoming a real capital city. Columbus in those days was basically a service city, and the main service was being provided to Ohio government and the regiment of lawyers, merchants, financiers, and others who did business in Columbus with the officeholders.

Finney by the 1840s had worked at one time or another as a cook, waiter, or servant for most of the major hostelries in town, and he was well liked and well known. What was not so well known was that he was also a runaway slave.

On March 27, 1846, Jerry Finney was persuaded to cross the river to Franklinton, where acting Justice of the Peace William Henderson promptly turned him over to a runaway slave hunter named Alexander Forbes. Despite Finney's protests and requests for a trial, he was placed in a carriage to Cincinnati, from where he was taken across the Ohio River and returned to his owner in Kentucky.

The way in which the popular Finney had been taken outraged many people in Columbus. And in short order, Henderson and four other men involved in the affair were arrested for kidnapping. In July 1846, these men and Forbes, the slave hunter, were indicted for unlawful seizure and other offenses.

The trial of these people in September of 1846 occupied

the attention of Columbus for several days and attracted national notice, as well. The prosecution was conducted by the county prosecutor, A.F. Perry, and a young lawyer named William Dennison. The defense consisted of F.J. Mathews and Noah Swayne, two of the best attorneys in Ohio, if not America, at the time.

Henderson was convicted by a jury and the other defendants were acquitted. Ultimately, Henderson's conviction was also reversed because of procedural errors during the trial. Using another approach, the Ohio Legislature retained the services of an attorney to try to gain freedom for Finney through the Kentucky courts. This effort also failed.

Finney was finally purchased from his owner and came to Columbus and freedom after being held in Kentucky for several months. But he returned a broken man, and died of a virulent lung infection within a short time.

But the Finney case had repercussions long after the death of the man who had fled slavery to what he thought was freedom in Ohio. Outraged by continuing "interferences" with their lives, Southerners insisted on a Fugitive Slave Law as part of the Compromise of 1850. This law requiring the return of southern runaways proved to be so "odious and despicable" to anti-slavery advocates that an illegal but effective "Underground Railroad" sprang up to assist fleeing slaves in their journey to freedom in Canada.

Columbus was a major "switching station" on that Underground Railroad. Dennison, the young prosecutor, went on to become a founder of the Republican Party, governor of Ohio, and Lincoln's Postmaster General. And the conflict which took more lives than any other in American history, became a little less "irrepressible" because a small group of men either did not know or did not care that men like Finney had friends as well.

The "Shot Tower" at Fort Hayes, c. 1885.
Courtesy of the Columbus Metropolitan Library.

52

~14~
Fort Hayes

The Civil War transformed Columbus as no event before or since. Over four long and bloody years, Ohio provided more soldiers and resources to the war effort than any other state in the Union. Many of the most successful leaders of the Union Army came from Ohio: Sherman, Sheridan, Custer, and Grant, to name a few. And Ohio withstood Confederate invasion, political opposition, and civilian outrage at the draft to earn Lincoln's observation that "Ohio has saved the Union!"

By the end of the Civil War, there were more soldiers in Columbus than citizens. Camp Chase, a Union Army mobilization and training center, alone held 26,000 troops. They were needed at that site on the far west side because Camp Chase also held one of the largest Confederate prisoner of war camps in the nation.

At the start of the war, Goodale Park was used as a camp, as well. And over the course of the war, a number of other camps were established: Camp Wade in Worthington, and Camp Thomas north of what is now The Ohio State University. Also Tod Barracks, an officer's enclave, and the old Arsenal on Main Street were also in continuous use during the war. But with the exception of the Arsenal and a few cemeteries, markers and monuments, all of these places are gone, swept aside by a growing city—all except one.

That place is Fort Hayes. Of course at the time it was built, it was not called Fort Hayes. That came in 1922. In late 1863, when work began on the facility, Rutherford B. Hayes— of Delaware, Fremont, Cincinnati, and points in between, was a successful but not particularly well-known soldier from Ohio with no inkling of the destiny that awaited him. As a quiet, unassuming and self-described "somewhat unexciting" person,

Hayes would probably have been more surprised than most to find a fort named after him.

In fact, for its first few years of existence, the post didn't really have a formal name. It was called "the depot," and "the arsenal," among other things, and it came into being because, quite simply, Columbus in 1863 had a plethora of guns, was making more every day, and needed a place to put them.

Congress had authorized the construction of another arsenal in Columbus at the outbreak of the war, but it took Ordnance Corps. Gen. Ebeneezer Buckingham two years to finally select a 70-acre tract just north of town on the road to Cleveland and near the Columbus and Newark Railroad for the new facility.

Called Neil's Woods, the land was covered with mature oak trees. Robert Neil, a local entrepreneur and early settler, had intended the uncut forest to eventually become a city park like nearby Goodale Park, but the needs of the Army took precedence and work began on the site.

Over the course of the next two years, a number of major buildings were completed. Most important of these was the "main storehouse." Designed to safely store powder, ammunition and weaponry, the three-story building is dominated by a large square tower containing a series of steps linking the various floors. Over the years, this feature has come to be mistakenly called the "Shot Tower."

In the days before rifled muskets, round shot was made by dropping hot lead a certain prescribed distance into a vat of cold water, making perfectly round balls for military use. And although the tower could have been used for this sort of thing, there is no evidence that it ever was, or was even intended to be, used for that purpose.

With the exception of the Main Building, all of the other original buildings at Fort Hayes are gone. Over the years they were replaced by other buildings designed to be used as officers' quarters, storerooms, and drill halls. Most of these buildings date from the period between 1880 and 1920, when the place was known as Columbus Barracks. Over the years, the site became more of an administrative and training center than an actual, working arsenal.

During every war since the Civil War, Fort Hayes has acted as a recruiting and training center. After the passage of the Selective Service Act just before World War II, it also acted as an induction center until the conclusion of the active draft in 1973. And even today, part of Fort Hayes continues to be used as a training center and headquarters for certain local military units.

But beginning in the 1960s, much of the site was declared to be surplus and its future was uncertain. Largely through the efforts of Jack Gibbs, a local educator, about half of the Fort Hayes site was acquired by the Columbus Board of Education to be used as an alternative school.

Today, a mixture of new buildings stand side by side with some of the most architecturally and historically significant buildings in the city. The "Main Storehouse" is listed on the National Register of Historic Places and has been faithfully renovated to be classroom and gallery space.

With its beautiful grounds and hundreds of young people in daily attendance, it would appear that Mr. Neil got his park, after all. Noting the use of the original state arsenal as a Cultural Arts Center, Columbus has the rare distinction of having not one, but two former fortresses now in active use by the arts.

And as the man who ended Reconstruction by finally removing Union troops from a defeated and occupied South, President Hayes would probably be pleased as well with the new uses of the place that bears his name.

James Andrew c. 1900.
Courtesy of the Columbus Metropolitan Library.

Installing a sewer line c. 1915.
Courtesy of the City of Columbus.

~15~
James Andrew—Pioneer Plumber

Most of us take indoor plumbing for granted, and with it the plumbers who come to keep it working from time to time. And while the carrying of water and other things by man-made piping is as old as civilization itself, it has generally been something that only the well-off could afford.

In its earliest days, the citizens of the pioneer community of Franklinton on the west bank of the Scioto and the later residents of the frontier capital of Columbus used small town and rural methods of obtaining water and disposing of sewage. Hand-dug wells were quite common since the water table in this part of central Ohio was quite near the surface. Similarly, hand-dug holes for waste and garbage disposal topped by small buildings variously called "privys" or "backhouses", among other things, were in the back yards of most pioneer homes. If the well ran dry or the privy filled up, the simple solution was to move to a new spot and dig again. This worked fine when one lived in a virtually unsettled wilderness with a few dozen other people.

But as towns grew in size, so too did the problems of water supply and sewage disposal. By the 1840s Columbus was a town of several thousand people living in close proximity to each other and there were only so many places one could sink a new well. As ravaging epidemics of cholera, typhoid and malarial fevers moved through the town with increasing frequency it became clear that both intercepting sewers and clean sources of water were needed. Much of the attention of government from the 1840s to the 1880s centered on providing these needed public improvements.

As the city developed sewage and water systems, the people who built them were not licensed professionals in sanitary work. This lack of professional standards was glaringly illustrated by the continuation of occasional epidemics caused by leaking water and sewer lines. But it was neither water nor sewage that brought the first professional plumber to Columbus. It was William Platt and the promise of a new way to make light.

William Platt was a pioneer settler of Columbus, having arrived as a child with his family from New England in 1817. He entered the jewelry business and by the late 1830s, his shop on High Street opposite the Statehouse was a regular stop for travelers and residents alike. Married to Fanny Hayes of Delaware, Platt supported a family of three daughters and a son quite well. By the late 1840s, he was well-enough off to leave the jewelry business and devote his time to real estate development and investment in promising new businesses. One of these was the Columbus Gas Company. By 1850, Platt was President of the company and laboring to convince Columbus officials to light the streets with gas and Columbus residents to do the same at home.

It was a tough sell. Even without competition from electricity, many people were scared to death of a combustible compound that one could not see, taste or touch. And a small number of exceptional but rather spectacular accidental explosions in various parts of the country did little to foster confidence.

In 1855, William Platt approached the problem with characteristic directness. Having outgrown his former home, Platt proposed to build a showplace mansion on a three-acre plot at the northeast corner of Cleveland Avenue and Broad Street. It would be thoroughly modern with complete inside plumbing and be illuminated with gas lighting. To do the work and do it properly, Platt enlisted the services of a professional plumber.

James Andrew had been born in Scotland in 1822. At the age of 17 he apprenticed with a company in Glasgow specializing in the manufacture and installation of piping and fixtures for plumbing purposes. Great Britain was somewhat ahead of the

United States in this field since its Industrial Revolution had occurred earlier and the large cities resulting from it needed sanitary remedies at an earlier date. Andrew worked in Scotland for six years before moving to the United States where he worked for another ten years developing a general plumbing business.

William Platt's home was finished in 1856, and it soon became a showplace. One of the few places in the city with inside running water, the home was also a living advertisement for the beauty and inexpensiveness of residential gas lighting. And all of the systems ran properly the first time. William Platt was pleased and impressed.

James Andrew was impressed as well. He saw unlimited opportunities in the growing capital city. Leaving New York behind, he moved permanently to Columbus and soon was the proprietor of a large company providing professional plumbing services to both business and residential customers.

By the time Andrew ended his career in the 1890s, he had been in continuous practice in Columbus for more than 41 years. He had provided plumbing service to hundreds of residences and for many of the more important commercial buildings in the city as well from his modest three-story offices at 38 West Town Street.

James Andrew had brought modern plumbing methods to Columbus and helped make what had been a craft into a profession. But his lasting contribution to the city was in the health of its citizens. Because of his work and the work of others like him, sanitary water and sewer lines led to a drastic reduction of epidemic disease in the city. And his work with gas and electric conduits led not only to the safe lighting of the city but a reduction in accidental fires as well. In short, the seldom seen work of James Andrew and the plumbers who followed him have made Columbus a better place.

General George Armstrong Custer c. 1865.
Courtesy of the National Archives and Records Administration.

~16~
The Day Custer's Luck Ran Out

It was a very hot day. The column of mounted men paused at the top of a barren ridge of scrub grass and looked down at the tree-lined river wending its way along the valley below. The leader of the column could not fail to notice as well the dozens of homes and hundreds of people scattered across the floor of the valley. Many of those people were armed and angry and in his way.

And it was at this point, in the quiet of the mid-afternoon of June 25, 1876, that George Armstrong Custer looked back over his exhausted men and horses who had been marching steadily for several days and made a fateful decision.

Three large columns of troops had been in pursuit of these elusive bands of Sioux, Cheyenne and Arapaho. The people had left their reservations and moved into the wild country of eastern Montana along the Breaks of the Missouri River. Now with troops closing in from three sides, the tribes banded closely together and moved south along the Little Big Horn River. The assembled villages along the river numbered more than 12,000 people.

Custer's orders were to find the Sioux but not necessarily to engage them unless it was seen to be advantageous to do so. With more than 650 men at his disposal, Custer set out to do just that. Arriving at the village with his force worn out and dazed from lack of sleep, Custer decided the time had come to be bold. Splitting his force into three parts, he sent Captain Frederick Benteen wide to flank the pony herd and drive it away from the camp. Supporting Benteen was Major Marcus Reno with a strong mounted column of his own. This left Custer with 224 men of his own including scouts, newspaper men and a few other civilians.

By 3:30 PM on June 25, choices had to be made. Believing Reno and Benteen to be riding to support him and the major columns of Gibbon, Terry, and Crook only a day away, Custer perhaps felt he had little to fear.

Unbeknownst to the commander, Benteen's flanking force had been attacked vigorously and forced to retreat back to the river. Here they met Reno's troops and swirled among them in disorder and disarray. Reno, shocked by the force of the battle and distracted by the blood spattered on his face and clothing from the nearby death of an Indian scout, fled back up the ridge with Benteen's men.

On the hilltop, the men dug in and awaited a Native American counterattack. Unyielding to requests to go to Custer's aid, Reno decided to stay put and ordered his men to do the same. Encircled now by ever increasing numbers of very angry warriors from the more than 3,600 combatants in the Indian camp, Custer is now outnumbered by more than 18 to one. For the next several hours into the late afternoon, Custer tries desperately to fight his way out but by late afternoon it is all over. Custer and his force have been wiped out and the remainder of the Seventh Cavalry will endure continuing attacks through the night. In the morning the Indians are gone and the major armed forces begin to arrive. They soon find the mutilated and savaged bodies of Custer's men and hastily bury them.

And what does any of this have to do with Columbus? Four of the men who fought there were natives of Columbus and Franklin County. As Captain Frederick Benteen's column fell back in disarray from the camp in the earliest stage of the fighting, one of the first men hit was Sergeant Miles Ohara of Company M. He had enlisted in Columbus in 1872 at the age of 21. Ohara had been promoted to Sergeant only two weeks before the battle. Shot through the breast, he died in the earliest stages of the battle.

As the troops of Benteen and Reno fought their way up the bluffs overlooking the river, one of the men who made it to the top and dug in was Private Thomas Graham. Graham had enlisted in the cavalry in 1872 at the age of 18. Surviving the battle, Graham would return to Columbus in his old age and die there in 1907.

With Custer's fighting force was Private Weston Harrington. Born in 1855 in rural Franklin County, Harrington had enlisted in 1872 in Columbus. He fell in battle halfway down the bluff in part of the swirling struggle to break out of the tightening trap. A grave marker in a small Prairie Township cemetery remembers the young man who died and was buried in faraway Montana.

And then there was First Sergeant Edwin Bobo. Born in 1845, Sergeant Bobo was an experienced combat soldier, a hard fighter, and one of the last men to die that day. He was later found near Captain Miles Keogh, whose horse, Comanche, was the only living survivor of Custer's detachment that day.

Finally there is one other combatant worthy of mention in the context of Columbus. Sergeant Stanislas Roy was born in Europe as were more than half the men in the Seventh Cavalry. He ended up on the hilltop with Reno and Benteen. During the long night following the battle, the attacks continued. Sergeant Roy "brought water to the wounded under the most galling fire of the enemy and at great danger to life." For this action, Sergeant Roy was one of several men of the Seventh Cavalry awarded the Congressional Medal of Honor in 1878. Sergeant Roy ultimately retired to Columbus, Ohio, where he died in February, 1913. He is buried in a local cemetery. The Battle of the Little Big Horn was a turning point in American history. Outraged by the defeat of a modern army and its controversial leader, political and military leaders came under intense pressure to subdue and control Native America.

Over the next 20 years, The United States did just that.The legacy of the Little Big Horn is a national reminder of who we once were and who we have become in the years since that struggle. It is also a reminder that the Seventh Cavalry came from everywhere in general and Columbus, Ohio, in particular.

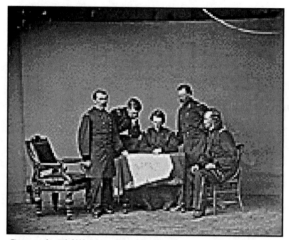

Generals Phillip H. Sheridan, George A. Custer,
Thomas C. Devin, James W. Forsyth, Wesley Merritt, c. 1863.
Courtesy of the National Archives and Records Administration.

General James W. Forsyth

He was born in Maumee City, Ohio, near Toledo, in 1836 to a family that was relatively well-off for that time. His father was closely acquainted with Lewis Cass, the frontier soldier and politician, and that acquaintance came in handy when young James sought a career in the military.

Forsyth received an appointment to West Point and did well in his academic work, making many friends who he would encounter again. The most important of these was a fiery and energetic Irishman from Somerset, Ohio, named Phil Sheridan. Forsyth left West Point with a Second Lieutenant's commission in 1858.

His first active service was on a small island named San Juan, off the coast of Oregon, whose ownership was in dispute with Great Britain. His immediate superior, George Pickett, later acquired some renown as a Confederate general during the Civil War.

By March 1861, Forsyth had been promoted to First Lieutenant. Then Fort Sumter fell in April, 1861, and the war that took more American lives than any other began in earnest. Forsyth was promoted to Captain and served for General George McClellan during several early campaigns in the war. By 1863, Forsyth had been promoted to Major, was cited for gallantry at the battle of Chickamauga, and had joined the staff of General Phil Sheridan.

Sheridan went west after the Civil War and became the chief military peace keeper on the moving frontier. Based in Chicago, Sheridan spent a great deal of his time on the move through the vast territory stretching west from the Mississippi. Marrying a daughter of former Governor William Dennison of Ohio, Forsyth had little time to see her since he was often on the trail with Sheridan.

Sheridan was a forthright and plainspoken man who cared little who he offended. Although he always denied it, he was reported by many witnesses to have once said that "the only good Indian is a dead Indian." And to show that he could offend his own countrymen as well, he once remarked, "If I owned Hell and Texas, I'd live in Hell and rent out Texas." This comment prompted one unreconstructed former Confederate to write that at least Sheridan was loyal to his place of origin.

James Forsyth stayed with Sheridan through the great campaigns against the Northern Cheyenne and the Red River War against the Comanche and Kiowa nations. In 1876, he went with Sheridan to the battlefield on the Little Big Horn where his old friend George Custer died with several hundred of his men.

By 1878, Forsyth had reached a point in his career where he could no longer stay on Sheridan's staff and advance in his career. So he left Sheridan and in time became the Colonel of the Seventh Cavalry, Custer's old regiment. Forsyth often said and his superiors agreed that his rebuilding of the Seventh after its shattering defeat at Little Big Horn was probably the best work of his career. By the late 1880s, the Seventh, which had lost more than a third of its men on one devastating day, was one of the best fighting units in the American Army.

By 1890, the opening of the Great West was coming to an end. The great herds of buffalo that had sustained the plains Indians were dwindling and the railroads which united East and West were bringing settlers and their way of life to the vast open spaces of the Great Plains. For the Lakota Sioux, a way of life was ending.

In December of 1890, a band of several hundred Sioux men, women, and children under the leadership of a man called Spotted Elk by his people and Big Foot by the soldiers and settlers, had been overtaken and detained by several companies of the Seventh Cavalry. On December 27, 1890, the Sioux were escorted to a camp along a creek called Wounded Knee. During the night James Forsyth arrived with more of the Seventh and took command.

The next morning, the Seventh Cavalry surrounded the

camp and trained a battery of Hotchkiss field artillery pieces on the camp. Ordered to disarm the Sioux, the cavalry was doing just that in a tense and hostile atmosphere when a shot rang out. The result was a full scale battle that rapidly deteriorated as the Hotchkiss Guns began to fling their two-inch shells at any Sioux in sight. By the time it was over, at least 150 Native Americans were dead and the Seventh Cavalry had 25 dead and 35 wounded.

Wounded Knee outraged friends of the Native American population of the United States, and Forsyth was court-martialed. Forsyth welcomed an investigation as he felt he would be vindicated. He was right. After a long and careful inquiry, Forsyth was cleared and restored to active service.

James Forsyth continued to serve in the American Army until 1897 when he retired with the rank of Major General. A man on the move for most of his adult life, Forsyth returned to his wife's hometown of Columbus, Ohio, to live out the rest of his days. One of his daughters had died, and another was living in Vancouver. His son was in the Army in Arizona. But his other daughter lived in Columbus with her husband.

For the next nine years, James Forsyth lived in small but well-appointed rooms in the Cumberland Apartments on Parsons Avenue. He was a member of the prestigious Columbus Club and was well-received in the polite society of Columbus. On October 25, 1906, he suffered a stroke and died.

Of all the generals who have lived for a time in Columbus, James Forsyth is probably one of the people who is remembered least. He should be remembered more.

Bishop Sylvester Rosecrans.
Courtesy of the Columbus Metropolitan Library.

The interior of St. Joseph's Cathedral c. 1890.
Courtesy of the Columbus Metropolitan Library.

~18~
Bishop Sylvester Rosecrans

When Sylvester Rosecrans was growing up in rural Ohio in the 1830s, he probably had the same daydreams as most young boys of that time and place. Among them was probably not to end his days as the first Roman Catholic bishop of Columbus. But that was the way things turned out.

It is difficult to understate the influence of his older brother William on the life of young Sylvester. While William went to West Point to pursue a career in the military, young Sylvester went to Kenyon College for a more traditional version of higher education. In 1845, William underwent a profound religious experience and embraced the Roman Catholic faith. At about the same time, young Sylvester was baptized into that faith as well.

William S. Rosecrans went on to become one of the more notable generals in the Union Army during the American Civil War. Sylvester left his other work aside and became even more strongly committed to the religious faith he had adopted. He decided to place his life fully in the service of the church. Leaving Kenyon, he went to St. John's College in Fordham, New York, and graduated from that school at the age of 20. With the guidance of the then Reverend John Purcell of Cincinnati, young Rosecrans went to Rome where he pursued his studies.

Returning to the United States, he was asked to head a new college being established by now Archbishop Purcell in Cincinnati. He operated the school for two years until the coming of the American Civil War forced the school to close. At that point Rosecrans became a personal assistant to the Archbishop. By 1862, Rosecrans had advanced to the position of Auxiliary Bishop of Cincinnati.

In 1867, he came to Columbus to assume the pastorate of St. Patrick's Church after Reverend Fitzgerald left to become

Bishop of Little Rock. He came with the understanding that when a new See of Columbus was created, he would be its bishop. As Auxiliary Bishop he had participated in the laying of a cornerstone for a cathedral in Columbus, but work on the cathedral had stalled as the process of creating the new office had slowed as well.

In 1868, letters from the Papacy creating the See of Columbus were received and Sylvester Rosecrans was established as its first bishop.

The Roman Catholic community of Columbus in the late 1860s was ready to welcome a new bishop. While Catholics had been living in Columbus ever since the area was settled after the conclusion of the Indian wars of the 1790s, the population was relatively small compared to the total population of the town until the 1830s. At that point, the completion of the Ohio Canal and the National Road opened Columbus and most of central Ohio to transportation and trade. With the trade came large numbers of immigrants as well. In particular, significant numbers of German and Irish immigrants came to Columbus and established themselves on the north and south ends of the city. A large number of these immigrants were Roman Catholics.

By the end of the Civil War, the Roman Catholic population was well-established in Columbus, having survived the anti-Catholic and anti-immigrant hysteria of the Know Nothing movement of the 1850s. But the unity stimulated by the Civil War and the enormous economic growth of the years after the conflict had left most of that bitter legacy behind and the church looked forward to a brighter future.

And while the new bishop busied himself with all of the tasks associated with administering a growing religious organization, it soon became clear that finishing the cathedral was particularly important to him. It took ten years to complete the task.

The original cathedral had been designed to be a brick

structure with a center tower near its front entrance. Covered over with earth, the original foundation walls were rebuilt and redesigned to support stone walls instead with a tower placed to the side of the main entrances. At 92 feet by 185 feet, the building at Broad and Fifth Streets rose more than 42 feet from the ground on walls of cut stone more than three feet thick at the base. The bishop's brother, General Rosecrans, offered advice and assistance on some of the more difficult engineering problems involved in constructing the building.

When completed, the building could seat 2,000 people and with its magnificent stained glass windows and simple furnishings was a living reminder of almost 2,000 years of religious history.

On October 20, 1878, St. Joseph's Cathedral was dedicated with appropriate ceremonies presided over by Archbishop Purcell of Cincinnati. It was an important event not only to the Church but to the City of Columbus as a whole. An elaborate reception was prepared at City Hall (where the Ohio Theater is today) and people from across the city regardless of religious belief attended the celebration.

In the midst of the celebration, at the high point of his career in Columbus, Bishop Rosecrans collapsed. Suffering from stomach ulcers for many years, the Bishop had characteristically shrugged off his pain while continuing with his work. But on the evening of October 20, he was the victim of a massive stomach hemorrhage. After receiving the last rites of the church, he died at 10:15 PM the following day.

Today, St. Joseph's Cathedral, carefully renovated and maintained on a continuing basis, is a magnificent symbol of the strength and continuity of the Roman Catholic Church in central Ohio. It is also the last resting place of its builder. Bishop Sylvester Rosecrans, the first bishop of Columbus, is buried in the crypt beneath the building.

Alexander Livingston.
Courtesy of Ed Lentz.

ALEXANDER W. LIVINGSTON
HOUSE
HAS BEEN PLACED ON THE
NATIONAL REGISTER
OF HISTORIC PLACES
BY THE UNITED STATES
DEPARTMENT OF THE INTERIOR

BUILT 1865

Plaque at Livingston's home in Reynoldsburg.
Photo courtesy of Ed Lentz.

~19~
Alexander Livingston

Alexander Livingston was one of those people who was almost perpetually curious and ambitious to improve his own condition as well. He spent most of his life in a determined quest to make what once had been thought to be a poisonous plant, the tomato, into one of the more desired vegetables in the gardens of the world. In 1842, in addition to everything else he was doing, he entered into the occasional employ of a local gardener to learn more about how to grow seeds for market. After about a year, the young man began growing seeds for resale on his own and started to experiment with vegetable varieties.

By 1849, Livingston was making enough money growing seeds for resale that he was able to buy a small 50-acre farm of his own in Truro Township. At about the same time, he acquired 400 boxes of seeds for resale on commission from his old employer, who had moved to Iowa and set up a seed business in that state. It was from this experience that he concluded that there might be a future in tomatoes.

This was a rather daring point of view for that time. For most of recorded history, the tomato had not had a very savory reputation. Originally rather poisonous, tomatoes were small, wrinkly and not terribly attractive. Over the centuries, edible tomatoes had been produced, but they were neither attractive nor tasty.

Alexander Livingston vowed to change all of that. Sensing from his seed sales experience that there was a market for tomatoes, Livingston began to experiment. For the next 15 years he grew the widest variety of tomatoes trying to find one type of attractive size and taste. He failed to do so.

In 1864, he changed his approach. Already making a decent living as a grower of seeds for resale, there was no reason why he had to continue with his experiments. But Alexander Livingston was convinced that he could grow a commercially viable tomato. After five more years of cross-breeding hardy types of tomatoes, he produced a product of uniform size, smooth surface, and good taste. He called it the Paragon Tomato and introduced it to public sale in 1870. It was an instant success and overnight, and Alexander Livingston achieved an international reputation as a tomato breeder.

Over the next quarter century, Livingston established himself as one of the great seed producers in America. Building on his original success, he produced more than ten other important commercial varieties of tomato, and lectured extensively to both professional and public audiences on the specifics of his work and on scientific agriculture in general.

By the end of the 19th century, tomato growing was big business in Reynoldsburg, as is reflected in this reminiscence of Fay May in 1938, which appeared in a 1995 issue of the *Courier* newsletter of the Reynoldsburg Truro Historical Society.

"When the tomatoes began to ripen, many men and boys were given work grinding them into pulp by hand and depositing into barrels in the fields where the pulp ripened for a few days, then it was loaded into wagons and hauled to the washer down at Blacklick Creek. The good seed went to the bottom, the light seed floated and was run off and then away. Also the pulp was wasted, and many a fortune was washed away down the creek, whereas today it would be made into catsup.

"Once the state fish commission said the tomato brine was killing the fish and ordered it kept out of the creek. We never knew if it killed any fish or not. We doubt it, for everyone around here half a century ago know that two men who were pals drank that brine from out of the barrels in the fields and were drunk all fall."

In 1880, Livingston relocated to Iowa to supervise the production and distribution of his product from seed farms and distribution centers in that more centrally located state. He left the business he had established in Columbus to the supervision of his children under the name of A. W. Livingston's Sons, Columbus.

By the time Alexander Livingston was in his 70s, he was recognized around the world as the virtual inventor of the tomato in its modern form. At the time of his death, companies like Heinz and Hunt were beginning to make their fortunes in processing for easy public use a tomato that only a few years before had been considered by many to be unfit for human consumption.

Alexander Livingston died on November 11, 1898, and is buried in Green Lawn Cemetery in Columbus.

Much of the information used in this article was gleaned from the previously published work of Cornelia Parkinson of Reynoldsburg. Her 1981 History of Reynoldsburg, Ohio is particularly informative, and her interest in local history, love of a good story and prodigious research is acknowledged with thanks.

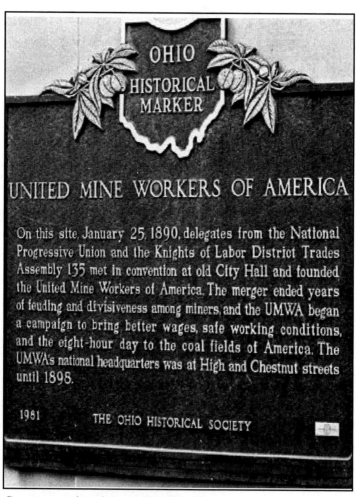

OHIO
HISTORICAL
MARKER

UNITED MINE WORKERS OF AMERICA

On this site, January 25, 1890, delegates from the National Progressive Union and the Knights of Labor District Trades Assembly 135 met in convention at old City Hall and founded the United Mine Workers of America. The merger ended years of feuding and divisiveness among miners, and the UMWA began a campaign to bring better wages, safe working conditions, and the eight-hour day to the coal fields of America. The UMWA's national headquarters was at High and Chestnut streets until 1898.

1981   THE OHIO HISTORICAL SOCIETY

Commemorative plaque at the Ohio Theatre.
Photo courtesy of Ed Lentz.

~20~
The United Mine Workers

It was nasty, dark, dirty, dangerous work. Men lay on their sides in pools of filthy water in a dank room only a few feet high lit by a candle or two, and hacked away with picks at the roof above them. When suitable holes were made, black powder blew out chunks of the roof to the floor where it was collected and hauled to the surface in carts pulled by men, boys and mules. This was coal mining about 150 years ago, and the methods and tools hadn't changed much in the previous 400. Men put their lives and health at risk in the lonely blackness of the mines for ten and 14 hours at a time and counted themselves fortunate to earn a dollar or two a day. It was a difficult life.

In the earliest days of Ohio's history, there had not been much mining at all. Stretching through the hill country of eastern and southeast Ohio were huge quantities of coal. But very few people went after it. As late as the 1840s, Ohio miners were only removing a few hundred thousand tons of coal a year and most of that was for local consumption.

There were a number of reasons why this was the case. Prior to the 1860s, most industry in Ohio and America was local industry. There was no really effective transportation network linking the West with the Midwest and most work of any kind was local work by local people for local markets.

And the fuel of choice for all of this work was wood. Ohio was largely covered with mature forests when settlers began coming here after the Indian Wars of the 1790s and our late unpleasantness with the British in the War of 1812. It seemed that there was no end to the forests, and their removal for fuel for industry served the valuable additional purpose of clearing the land for further agricultural development.

But eventually the arrival of canals, decent roads, and

railroads meant that the resources and products of Ohio could be shipped anywhere in the United States—or for that matter the world—and they were.

Furthermore, the developing iron and steel industries were finding that coal provided a cheap and abundant alternate fuel resource to wood.

So from the Mahoning River Valley in the northeast to the Hocking Valley in the south, coal began to be mined in ever greater quantities. By 1885 18,000 men were mining more than 8,000,000 tons of coal a year.

Some of these men, and almost without exception they were men, were people from England, Wales and Scotland whose families had mined coal for hundreds of years in their homelands. Others were newly arrived immigrants from Ireland, Germany, and elsewhere in Europe seeking a new start in a new land. Still others were the sons and heirs of the frontier families who had carved homes from the wilderness and were now seeking a new life of their own.

Fiercely loyal one to another, the miners considered themselves highly skilled craftsmen who risked their lives daily in a way of life that had changed little since the end of the Middle Ages. If the mine didn't collapse and kill, then opening a pocket of noxious gas with nowhere to run might do the job just as well. And if by luck and pluck one survived these obvious dangers, and most men did, there was still the grueling work, the onset of rheumatism from working constantly in the wet and the slow suffocation from breathing coal dust, called "black lung."

But if life was tough, it soon was to get tougher. The same transportation and industrial revolution that created the demand for coal also made coal mining itself into big business with huge corporations increasingly dominating the field. These companies established entire towns in the hills and valleys, whose major business was the production of coal. And increasingly that mining was being done with machines.

In Columbus, a man named Joseph Jeffrey had left banking and begun making coal mining equipment in the 1870s. By the turn of the century the Jeffrey Mining and Manufacturing Company was one of the biggest manufacturers of coal mining equipment in the world and one of the major industries in the capital city.

All of this meant that the local associations and unions of miners and mine laborers, which had served the needs of local mines for many years, perceived themselves to be increasingly less effective.

To counter this trend, it came to be felt that a truly national organization of miners was needed.

In 1890, representatives of several local and regional miners groups came together in Columbus, Ohio, and formed the United Mine Workers of America. It was no accident that they chose Columbus.

Columbus was an easily accessible town by railroad from just about anywhere in the United States and was promoting itself effectively as THE place for meetings and conventions. Also, Ohio and Pennsylvania were the coal mining centers of America and many of the delegates were from that part of the world. More importantly, Ohio was the industrial and political linchpin of America in the era after the Civil War. Ohio was producing more coal, steel and presidents than any other state in the Union in those days. Ohio's capital was a great place to get attention.

So in their best Sunday suits, the assembled delegates gathered on the Statehouse steps and posed for their formal portrait. Ahead was a century of work that would often have as many defeats as victories. But on that day in January, 1890, something new in the story of America's mine workers began.

Looking east on Broad Street, c. 1910.
Courtesy of the Columbus Metropolitan Library.

~21~
East Dream Street

There is something in all of us, I suppose, that would like to return to a time and place that seemed to be somehow better and less troubling than the world we live in now. Part of our fascination with the past is our continuing search for such a place. In Columbus, at the turn of the century, one of those places was East Broad Street.

You are looking east on Broad Street. From the Statehouse to Franklin Park, the entire street was lined with what one writer of the period called the "Handsome Homes of Columbus." Here lived the people who had made it and knew they had made it; the people who were still trying to make it; and the people who had made it, lost it, but still were hanging on to the shadow if not the   substance of accomplishment.

Broad Street emerged in the mid-1800s as the pre-eminent address in Columbus by a quirk in transportation history. The original east-west streets of downtown Columbus all received equal use since they were all equally impassable dirt tracks once one left the area around the Statehouse.

This all changed when the National Road (U.S. Route 40) reached Columbus in the early 1830s. The National Road entered the city on Main Street from the east. It was originally planned to leave town by the same street. But High Street merchants complained that their businesses would be destroyed if this happened. So the route of the National Road turned north from Main onto High Street. It then turned west at Broad Street and followed that road out of the city.

With that development, East Broad Street was spared most of the heavy traffic that moved elsewhere through the city. As early as 1837, Alfred Kelley had built a mansion "way out in the country" near the spot where COSI stood for many years. In the years that followed, a number of other people followed him. By the 1850s, the street was well built up out to the city limits at East Public Lane (Parsons Avenue). But there was not much past that point. The Taylor family built their mansion during this period farther out along Broad Street near Alum Creek. But there was not much between them and the houses on the other side of Parsons Avenue.

All of this changed after the Civil War. The war had provided an enormous economic boost to American industry, and government spending on railroads had literally tied the country together east of the Mississippi. Emerging from the conflict, Columbus became an industrial center. It also became a city rather than an overgrown small town.

And while the development of Broad Street continued apace, growth was somewhat stalled by the commanding presence of the Central Ohio Lunatic Asylum which took up three city blocks near Parsons and Broad. And the rather large pond near Eighteenth and Broad tended to slow people down as well.

In January 1868, some of this impediment to the march of housing for the well-to-do was rather abruptly eliminated with a spectacular fire which killed dozens of people and burned the institution to the ground. When it was originally built in the 1830s, the state had confidently placed the Asylum "far away from the town" to insure that the beneficial aspects of rural life could be experienced by the unfortunate inmates. By the time of the fire, the Asylum—like the Deaf School, the Blind School, and the Pentientiary—was squarely in the middle of the city. Unlike the other institutions, the Trustees of the Asylum chose not to stay in the city. Instead they moved once again to the country and occupied the heights to the west of the city overlooking Sullivant's Prairie. Today that area is called the Hilltop.

Into the vacuum left by the departure of the institution stepped two real estate developers who planned and opened the East Park Place addition. The subdivision consisted of three long north-south streets, each of which contained a long elliptical park in the middle of the block. The streets were patriotically named Hamilton, Jefferson and Lexington. East Park Place was THE place to live in the 1870s. In later years, more modest homes were built in the development. One of them became the boyhood home of James Thurber and has been nicely restored. Still later, Lexington Avenue was removed to make way for Interstate 71, but the other two park-like streets still remain.

In 1888, William Graham Deshler visited Havana. The son of the founder and heir-apparent to the Deshler banking empire was impressed with the tree-lined streets of the Cuban capital. When he returned to Columbus, he made an offer to the civic leadership of his hometown. If the city would provide the land, he would provide the trees. They did—and he did. By 1890, Broad Street was lined with a double row of trees from downtown to Franklin Park. The street was called "Judges Row" and was one of the most fashionable residential streets in America. Over the years, the trees began to suffer from disease, exhaust fumes, and occasional accidents. By the 1930s they were gone. As the downtown grew, Broad Street began to lose its charm. After the end of World War II, dozens of familes left their old family homes and moved to the suburbs. Many of the mansions were torn down. Others were converted to business use.

Only in recent years has the continued loss of these homes slowed to a stop due to the active efforts of local neighborhood groups, historical organizations and a new generation of people who like to live and work in these great old buildings. There has even been recent talk of replacing the trees along the avenue. William Graham Deshler would be pleased, and I suspect, so would the rest of us.

P.W. Huntington, c. 1900.
Courtesy of the Columbus Metropolitan Library.

~22~
P.W. Huntington

Over the course of the history of banking in central Ohio, there were a number of institutions whose founders solved the problem of what to call the place by simply, with pardonable pride, naming the place after themselves. There was a Rickley Bank, and a Reinhard Bank, and a Hayden Bank and several Deshler Banks. Most of them are gone now, lost to the great corporate merger mania of the banking business of this century. Except one—P. W. Huntington's bank lives on as the Huntington National Bank. This story is partly about that bank but mostly it is about the man who made it.

Peletiah Webster Huntington was born in 1837 to a truly old New England family. The Huntingtons had been in Norwich, Connecticut, since 1659. And at last look, there are still some of them there. His father had been a banker, and a forebear for whom he was named had helped finance the American Revolution. But the young man was less sure about his future. Like many young men from New England, he went to sea to find himself. After two years of the nautical life, he drifted a bit before ending up in Columbus working as a messenger for the Ohio State Bank.

Messengers then as now did not make much. But Huntington was a quick study and liked the quickly growing capital city. Columbus in the 1850s was changing rapidly as large numbers of German and Irish immigrants arrived by train, road and canal to turn the frontier village into the commercial center of central Ohio.

He made the acquaintance and earned the friendship of another remarkable man—David Deshler. Deshler was a former cabinet maker who many thought to be quite foolish to pay $1000 for a town lot in 1818 when most lots could be had for $100 or less.

It was near the northwest corner of Broad and High and Deshler thought it might one day be worth something. He was right.

He was also correct in assuming that there had to be a better way to make a living than building bookshelves for local customers. He decided to go into banking. And he was very good at it indeed. By 1866, Deshler, always looking for bright, young talent to help him continue to build his fortune, found P. W. Huntington. He helped the young man set up a new banking company called simply P. W. Huntington & Co. in a Deshler-owned building near Broad and High.

In those days before government regulation, all one really needed to set up a bank was some capital and the trust of at least some of one's neighbors. Deshler provided the former and Huntington the latter. Soon the company was making money and doing quite well indeed.

P. W. Huntington liked the corner of Broad and High and by the 1870s had established himself on the southwest corner of the intersection in an ornate castle-like banking building. Each day he walked to work from his home at 125 East Broad Street where the National City Bank is today to his office at Broad and High. Along the way he would stop to talk with his old friends and introduce himself to new ones. He liked to do his own marketing from time to time in the Old Central Market on South Fourth Street for the same reason.

P. W. Huntington was successful because he strongly believed that people needed to give back as much as they received from their community. He served on the boards of numerous corporations but spent as much or more time with local nonprofit groups as well. He was treasurer of the Green Lawn Cemetery Association for 37 years and was largely responsible for getting its chapel built. He provided the organ to the completed building. He endowed a music alcove in the

Columbus Public Library and stocked it with materials from his own private collection. He was a charter member of the Columbus Oratorio Society and the Columbus Club, which he served as President.

He was married three times in a time when childbirth and disease often killed women at a much earlier age than their husbands. His children by each of the marriages would go on to careers and lives as varied as the interests of their father. By the time he died in 1918, he had been retired from the banking business for four years, leaving his bank in the capable hands of the next generation of his family and a group of trusted associates.

P. W. Huntington never lost his interest in the people of his adopted town. For most of his career he continued to walk to work winter and summer, thriftily collecting fallen dead wood from the trees along Broad Street and Statehouse Square for his office wood stove. On a pleasant day he could often be seen sitting in his shirtsleeves on the front steps of his bank whittling on one of those pieces of wood while he talked to passersby. On such days, P. W. Huntington was still a man of integrity and resolution. But he was not that formidable at all.

There is very little left of P. W. Huntington's original bank today. The institution moved down the street first to the Huntington Building and then to the nearby Huntington Center. The building at the corner was torn down and nothing remained of it except its basement. In recent years that basement has been operated as a restaurant under differing names where, among other things, one could dine near the former vault of Mr. Huntington's bank.

From time to time as I walk through the downtown I come across a stick or small branch of wood which has been washed into a gutter by recent rain. I usually leave it for P. W. Huntington at Broad and High as a reminder to him and myself that, while much has changed in Columbus over the years, some very important things have not changed at all.

Emil Ambos's gravestone in Green Lawn Cemetery.
Photo courtesy of Ed Lentz.

23

Emil Ambos

Every place that I know of has at least a few characters who stride across the historical stage and who seem just a little bit better, or worse as the case may be, than the rest of us. Sometimes these memorable figures have had their real story embellished and elaborated in subsequent retelling to the point where their story ceases being history and becomes the stuff that legends are made of.

And then there are people like Emil Ambos. He too is a legend in Columbus in his own way. And I suppose that if we looked closely, we would find that he was just as courageous and honorable as many and more so than most. But that is not why we remember him today.

Emil Ambos, more than most of the people of his time, knew that a rich life was something far different than a wealthy life. He had the knack of making a living by helping his fellow citizens live well. And in so doing, he lived pretty well himself. He learned first hand from his parents both how to make money and that the money one made was not the most important thing in life.

Peter Ambos was a young German immigrant who had arrived in America virtually penniless. He had scratched and saved enough money in a few years to move west with the constant stream of people who were looking to find a new future in a new country. By the time, he got to Columbus in 1830, the town looked like it might have a future for him.

The secret of Peter Ambos's success was that he made a product that most people didn't really need but couldn't do without. Peter Ambos did not make clothes or shoes or nails. He made candy.

Peter Ambos opened a candy store and restaurant on High Street between Town and Rich Streets. Soon he moved to a location directly across from the Capitol on High. He was successful because he tried to be somewhat ahead of his time. In addition to his candy, Peter Ambos brought the first oysters to the city for the amusement and pleasure of his customers. They came by stagecoach sealed in large metal cans and created a sensation. Peter Ambos also remembered his German roots and introduced the first public Christmas tree to the city.

Along the way he married Dorothea Jaeger in 1841. Her family had also prospered in the new country. Her father, Christian Jaeger, was an officer in the Austrian army and had stopped in Columbus in 1833 because he heard there was cholera farther west. He stayed in Columbus and by the 1840s was one of the more prosperous Germans in Columbus.

The Ambos family built a fine home on South High Street which became something of a showplace in the South End. It was into this world of unpretentious prosperity that Emil Ambos was born. His father, with characteristic practicality, sent his son to college to improve his mind and trained him as a carriage painter so he would always have a trade to practice if necessary.

Emil did not become a carriage painter. As the sole surviving child of the family, Emil ultimately inherited the candy business, the restaurant, and several other enterprises. He added to the family fortune by developing a successful wholesale liquor business.

But Emil Ambos did not become one of the more memorable people in Columbus because of the way he worked. He became famous because of the way he lived.

Emil Ambos never married but that never deterred his active social life. He acquired a three-story building on Town Street just east of High in the heart of the business district and made it over into a rather interesting bachelor's apartment with parlors, reception rooms and one of the better-equipped game rooms in Columbus. A lifelong lover of horses, he had a rather elaborate stable built behind his home. And since his bedroom was on the second floor, he put the horses on the second floor of the stable as well, with a bridge connecting his room to theirs.

His rural estate was known as Ambos Pleasure Farm and was located near Canal Winchester. It featured a practice track for his horses, a five-room cottage and not one but two fishing lakes. This was because the great passion of Emil Ambos's life was fishing. One of the lakes featured a steam powered yacht for excursions, and the other had a small island with a log cabin.

To his various homes and properties, Emil Ambos brought an almost continuous stream of friends, relative and acquaintances. He also organized excursions for local schools and for hundreds of underprivileged children each year. To more than two generations of Columbus residents, he was 'Uncle Am', the man with a pocket full of candy, a ready smile, and a great heart.

Emil Ambos observed on one occasion that Statehouse Square somehow always looked a little lifeless even with its trees and monuments. And then he saw why. Except for a few birds, there was nothing living on the square. The growth of the city had forced all of the forest animals away. He solved this problem by importing squirrels from his farm and letting them loose in the trees on the square from time to time.

And when Emil Ambos died, he had already determined that he wanted his grave marker to be memorable as well. If ever you visit Green Lawn Cemetery, you will find Emil Ambos on the south side of the lake in the middle of the grounds. Unimpressed by traditional monuments, he commissioned a lifesize bronze statue of himself sitting by a stream in his fishing clothes. Even today Emil Ambos continues to remind us that living well is what living is about.

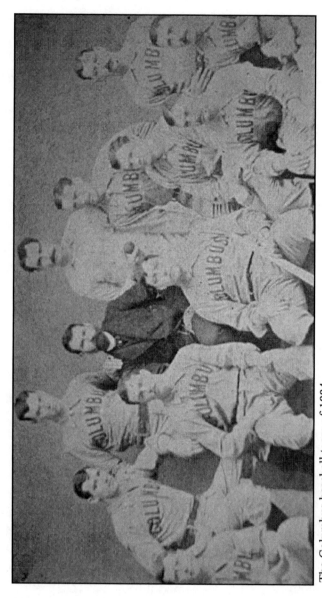

The Columbus baseball team of 1884.
Courtesy of the Columbus Metropolitan Library.

24

The Baseball Team of 1884

It took more than half a century for baseball to become America's game. From rather humble beginnings as an alternative to several other games in the early 1800s, the game of baseball began to capture the imagination and the leisure time of hundreds of thousands of American young people, and their parents, in the years before and shortly after the American Civil War.

But with the passing of the frontier came both a modest increase in leisure time and opportunities to spend it in new ways. The first theatre in Columbus opened in the early 1830s coincidental with the arrival of the National Road and the Ohio Canal. And both commercial and voluntary organizations dedicated to art, literature, and music were not far behind. By the end of the Civil War in 1865, Columbus was well-linked with the rest of the country by telegraph, railroad and regular mail and package delivery services. With this connection came the ability to follow national trends in dress, politics, society and leisure activity. And the sport which most people, young and old—men especially but women as well—followed most closely was baseball.

Why was that the case? Fans of the game, and even occasional philosophers and social critics, have pondered that point for more than a century. And some of their observations have led to a few conclusions. Baseball is an easy game to follow and to learn to play initially. But it is also a game which can be analyzed to death, studied in infinite detail, and whose winning strategies can be as subtle as those of Lee at Chancellorsville or Napoleon at Austerlitz. In short, it is a game that can be followed either casually or closely.

It is also a game that does not require great expense to play. Today even Little League baseball occurs in modern well-lit fields made especially for the game, played by young players outfitted in uniforms with safety protection and equipment made of plastics and metals that could and probably did contribute to the success of the space program. But what does it really take to play baseball—a bunch of people, a bat, a ball and a modest size place in which to play. This is the essence of the success of baseball—one can play it just about anywhere, with just about anyone, and have a good time without running the risk of getting seriously maimed in the process. In that sense it certainly beats bear-baiting or running the gauntlet—two of the more interesting participant sports of the frontier era.

So who were these boys of the summer of 1884? In a few words, they were one of the most successful baseball teams Columbus has ever produced. In an era when professional baseball was just beginning to emerge from its amateur origins, the 1884 team scored an impressive number of victories and came very close to winning the pennant in the American Association. They were a group of likable young men who captured the hearts and imagination of Columbus. And then the season ended.

Over the next several years, fans and entrpreneurs tried to sustain and foster professional baseball in Columbus but with a notable lack of economic success. It would not be until well into the 20th Century that the success of minor league teams like the Columbus Redbirds, Jets, and Clippers combined with the popularity of college baseball at The Ohio State University and other area schools would make baseball a permanent professional spectator sport in the Columbus community.

But what happened to the popular team of 1884 who came so tantalizingly close to victory? In a society that often dwells on today's victor and tomorrow's prospects, we often do not look back to see what became of yesterday's heroes.

In 1899, a reporter decided to find out what happened to the 1884 team and where all of these fellows were 15 years later. This is what he found, from left to right in the photograph that accompanies this story.

"Ed Morris, pitcher, keeps a saloon in Allegheny, Pennsylvania; Tom Brown, right field, recently appointed an umpire of the National League; Jimmy Field, first base, first and captain—Buffalo club; Fred Carroll, catcher, lives in San Francisco, not playing; Gus Schmelz, manager, managing Minneapolis club; Frank Mountain, pitcher, gents' furnishing goods business, Schenectady, NY; Rudolph Kemmler, catcher, not playing, living in Chicago; Charley Smith, second base, Binghamton, NY—relieved from diamond; Edward Dundon, pitcher, dead; William Kuehne, third base, managing a small team somewhere in Canada; John Richmond, shortstop, not playing—living in Philadephia. Fred Mann, not playing, lives in Manchester, New Hampshire."

The only thing not clear from the description is what exactly happened to Charley Smith when he was "relieved from diamond." There are two interesting things to notice about this group. Four of the twelve in 1899, 30% of the team, are still directly involved in the game of baseball. And not a single one of them is working in Columbus. Perhaps there are important and profound truths to be gleaned from these observations. Certainly a trip to the ball park will help make it clear exactly what they are. We will let you know.

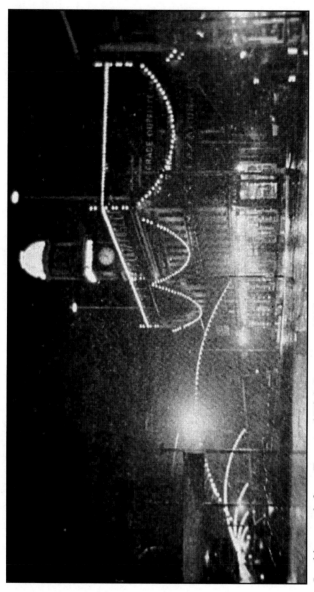

Looking south from Town and High Streets, c. 1898.
Courtesy of the Columbus Metropolitan Library.

96

~25~
Arch City

We are standing at the corner of Town and High Streets looking south. It is about 1898 and the view is from a popular photograph of that era, which can still be found without too much trouble. Columbus in those days was known as "Arch City." A little girl visiting Columbus for the first time wrote, "High Street at night is like a fairyland!" It is easy to see why. But where did these arches come from?

The Grand Army of the Republic was THE social and political organization for Union Army veterans in the years after the Civil War. Their annual reunions were big business and drew tens of thousands of former soldiers and their families for a week of marching, meeting, and general camaraderie. In 1888, The GAR came to Columbus. The town of 80,000 people played host to 250,000 tourists for ten days. Where did we put them? We put them in tent cities on the site of what is now Fort Hayes, and other open sites around the city. The city of Columbus picked up, cleaned up, and generally dressed itself up for the occasion. But not content with being simply neat and clean, the town also decided to do something special for the veterans.

Something special in this case was a series of wooden arches lit with gaslights that ran down High Street from where the Convention Center stands today all the way to the Courthouse complex at Fulton and High. The arches turned High Street into a summer evening wonderland. For ten days, the sun never seemed to set on High Street.

There was a practical reason for all of this. The large gathering of veterans drew every thief, mugger, and con man within easy traveling distance to Columbus. And Columbus, like most cities, was not well-established as a place for late night promenading.

The city used oil, coal or wood for light as well as heat in its homes and factories, and there was usually a pall of thick black smoke hanging over the city. Further, inefficient sewers and an abundance of unhousebroken horses meant that one crossed streets at night with considerable caution. All of this meant that light was needed for reasons of safety during the GAR convention. Not overlooked, of course, was the idea that people who could see where they were going might stay out later and spend more money at local merchants.

And that is precisely what happened. The veterans came in droves and liked what they saw. The GAR meeting of 1888 drew more people than any other meeting of Union Veterans except the Grand Review in Washington at war's end in 1865.

By September of 1888, when the event ended, everybody was happy. The vets were happy, local merchants were happy, and the public in general was happy. About the only people who weren't happy were the thieves and other criminal types who ended up spending most of the convention in jail.

The city decided to keep the lighted arches. They replaced the wooden arches with metal and the gaslamps with electric lights. This example was copied by a number of stores who lit up their fronts at night as well. In the background of the postcard, one can see the illumiminated front of the F & R Lazarus Co. At that time, the store was located on the block to the south of its present location.

To complete the effect the local street car company electrified itself in 1893 and used the arches to carry their power lines. They also added an excursion car called the Electra to its High Street line. The Electra was lit with dozens of tiny electric bulbs which made for a certain traffic-stopping effect as it came up the street. The lights on the front of the car formed a large five-pointed star which could be made to blink on request.

Most of what one can see in this picture is gone now. Lazarus moved to its new store in 1909. The arches came down in 1914. The streetcars were replaced first by trolley buses and then by motorcoaches. And over the years most of the buildings were torn down and replaced.

But not all of them. To the right of the picture stand three small buildings which have managed to survive from that time to our own. Stand at the corner leaning against one of those buildings and look south to the City Center Walkway some evening. If you look glancingly at that tunnel of light down the street, you can almost see the arches and some of what Columbus used to be.

Lutz's Tonsorial Parlor, c. 1898.
Courtesy of the Columbus Metropolitan Library.

26

Lutz's Tonsorial Parlor

I have been convinced for some time that a good barber is one of the noblest works of creation. If you think about it a bit, it takes a very special kind of person to be able to work with sharp implements in very close proximity to people with the widest variety of opinions, behavioral quirks, and standards of personal hygiene without either going crazy or getting killed. Barbers do this on a daily basis.

And they have done it for a long, long time.

Barbers of the past several centuries have evolved into people who help the rest of us look relatively presentable to the world. In the past they did a lot more than that. Emerging from the Middle Ages, when modern medicine was still defining itself, barbershops were also places where wounds could be cleaned and dressed and indeed where minor surgery of all sorts could be performed as well. As late as the last century, if one could not find a dentist, one went to a barber to have a tooth removed.

Eventually, as the modern professions of medicine, dentistry and nursing came more into their own in the wake of the Industrial Revolution in Western Europe and America, the barbershop evolved into something more like what it is today.

In the photo, we can see a glimpse of just what that was.

This is Fred Lutz's Tonsorial Parlor in 1898. A tonsorial parlor takes its name from the tonsure or distinctive hair treatment given to monks and clerics in Medieval Europe, and thereby implies a place where personal appearance is maintained or enhanced. This particular tonsorial parlor was located in the Goodale Hotel, directly across High Street from the State Capitol, near the spot where the Huntington Center and Riffe State Office Tower stands today.

Looking at the picture, we will see there are some notable differences between the shop of a century ago and one from our own time. Along the floor in strategic spots are spittoons to handle the dregs from one's chewing tobacco, a favorite masculine pastime of that period. Today water is easily available near every barber chair in most shops. This was not the case in this relatively upscale shop. Inside plumbing was still something of a luxury and the central sinks in the middle of the shop met the shampooing and other needs of all and sundry. And the shop is not that well lit. Today barbershops are quite well lighted and very bright and cheery in appearance. Even with the assistance of flash powder, Fred Lutz's establishment is still rather dark.

We note as well that most of the clientele is virtually horizontal in their respective barber chairs. This is not the way most people spend time in the chair today. The reason for this is that the basic tonsorial treatment of the period was a haircut and shave for 'two-bits' (25 cents). And since shaving, then and now, was done with a very sharp straight razor, most barbers wanted their client to be as immobile and accessible as possible.

Having said all of this, there is a lot in this century-old picture to remind us that much has not changed in the American barbershop. This is a male preserve. For most of our history, men had barbershops and eventually women had beauty parlors. And the two were not to be confused one with the other.

In most towns and in most neighborhoods, the barbershop is still pretty much a male preserve. It is here that young men and old gather on a regular basis to hear the news of the world and of each other's lives. It is a place where language and manners and customs are often bereft of the correctness associated with polite society. And it is a place where rites of passage like a first haircut or a trim before the big dance are excruciatingly endured by the recipient and observed with benign amusement by the assembled multitude.

Barbershops are the kind of places where male bonding is defined in this country.

They have also offered a wide variety of services other than purely tonsorial assistance. Fred Lutz was proud to offer sea salt baths to his clientele. It may strike us a little strange today that people would actually pay to end up smelling like they had fallen into Boston Harbor. But in a period when most folks only bathed infrequently at best, and when "taking the waters" at a spa or resort was considered quite healthful, a sea salt bath was considered not only hygienic but positively therapeutic as well.

In our own time, barbershops have also offered tanning machines, exercise equipment and a variety of other currently fashionable services to a waiting world.

Today the line between barber shop and beauty parlor has blurred somewhat with 'unisex' establishments and the simple fact that most barbers and beauticians will meet the needs of just about anyone who is intrepid enough to request service and has the wherewithal to pay for it.

But to many of us, a good barber once found is a treasure to be cherished. In the place where I live there are many nearby fine barbershops. But I still drive 20 miles or more from time to time to get a haircut from the one person I have found who really knows how to cut my hair. I hope he lives forever.

And in that view, I am sure I am not alone.

Sewer workers, 1930.
Courtesy of the City of Columbus.

27

The Sewers

Columbus existed for more than 30 years without sewers. In the course of that time its population grew from 500 people to more than 8,000. And for every person in town there were at least one or two horses, cows, sheep, dogs and even an occasional pet bobcat. All of these people and livestock generated an enormous amount of what one writer of the period euphemistically called "animal and vegetable waste."

Some of this waste was deposited in backyard privys or trashpits. Some was deposited in what residents called "gutters" but were really little more than shallow ditches on each side of the unpaved streets in the town. And some material, especially from businesses and stables and the like, was actually trucked to the river and dumped—thereby enriching the lives of the residents of Circleville and points south.

By 1848, this situation had become intolerable. Several local institutions joined with the city in financing a three-and-a-half foot sewer, which ran under Broad Street from the river to Jefferson Avenue. Constructed of brick and buried 18 feet deep, the sewer did its job quite well for more than 100 years. It was bypassed by later improvements, but most of the sewer still carries the weight of the street above it quite well. A notable exception to that resilience was a 20-foot section which collapsed under a rather surprised but uninjured motorist in a Mercedes some years ago.

And while this early effort at sewer construction seemed to work well, the same cannot be said for the projects which followed it over the next 40 or 50 years. In 1852, the rather large creek that gave Spring Street its name was enclosed in a covered sewer. This was viewed as a notable improvement since prior to that time, one crossed the street on foot bridges set at the major intersections. But by 1855, this sewer was leaking so badly that every basement along the street was knee-deep in rather foul-smelling water.

At the end of the Civil War, a "sewerage commission" reported that the laying of sewer lines in the city had no rhyme or reason. The lines did not connect one with another and whole parts of the downtown were not served at all. The answer to the problem was a new series of large "trunk" sewer lines which themselves would be connected to an "intercepting sewer" which would empty into the Scioto well below town. It was a logical, simple, and forthright solution to a difficult problem. If the recommendations had been implemented in a sound, work-manlike way, the result would have been helpful. They weren't, and the result was a nightmare.

The South End Sewer, draining most of what is now German Village, was so riddled with leaks that most of the wells along its route went dry as they drained into the adjacent sewer. The Fourth Street Sewer collapsed along 400 feet of its route shortly after its completion. But the most exasperating problem occurred in the Brewery district south of town.

The original idea had been to build a sewer which picked up the contents of most of the downtown sewers and run it parallel to the Scioto until it emptied into the River well below town. Fearing lawsuits by property owners outside town, the city stopped the project after it crossed the Ohio Canal near the breweries and let it empty into the river at that point. That point happened to be a rather flat flood plain which rapidly became, in the words of City Engineer John Graham, "an elon-gated cesspool emitting disagreeable and pestilential odors along its entire line for a distance of nearly a mile."

Responding to this challenge, city officials built yet

another set of trunk line sewers serving the continuously growing city in the 1880s. This project was supposed to cost $150,000—an enormous sum for that period. It ended up costing $350,000.

An investigatory report of the period explained why. "The Council and its officers, it seems, did not know that lumber would be required in making the excavation. They did not know a superintendent would be necessary. They did not know that the quality of water supplied to the city would be affected by discharging a main sewer into the river above and near the waterworks. They did not know that the discharge of a main sewer into Alum Creek, just west of the Lutheran College, would render its buildings uninhabitable." Another writer from the same period concluded that "All of which suggests the importance of choosing municipal officials on the basis of qualifications rather than that of political belief."

This cut to the core of the problem. Sewers were a political pawn in the 19th Century. Partisan politics was largely governed by the spoils system in Columbus, and some of the most important spoils were the lucrative paving, construction, and repair contracts handed out by city officials to their friends and supporters. The main reason the sewers were built haphazardly and quickly was that the builders were non-professionals trying to complete the work as quickly as possible.

All of this began to change with the emergence of engineering as a profession and the rise of non-partisan capital improvement construction projects in the early 1900s. For the past 80 years or so, sewer construction and maintenance has been so efficient and effective that we view a sewer failure as an unusual event. And while that is as it should be, we often forget to thank the people who build and maintain the system we cannot see but without which, our city simply would not be.

Columbus Home for the Aged.
Photo courtesy of Ed Lentz.

28

The Columbus Home for the Aged

Columbus, like most cities in our country, had a very straight-forward approach to dealing with the problems of the elderly for most of its early history. It did not do much about it.

From the time Columbus was founded in 1812 until well into its early history, most assistance to the unfortunate was predicated on the alleviation or remedying of a physical or social condition. For the poor and absolutely destitute there was the poor house or "county home" as it was euphemistically called. But unless one was an orphan or other sort of ward of the court, there was little in the way of public assistance for the very young or very old of Columbus.

With the arrival of the canal and the National Road in the 1830s this began to change. While most children and very aged persons continued to be cared for in the homes of families or friends, there began to emerge new classes of people who nobody wanted to take in.

As travelers moved across the Midwest heading for the new country to the west, young women were sometimes left behind by their families at the nearest town so that their relatives might continue their journey. The Columbus Female Benevolent Society was founded to deal with the people who found Columbus to be that nearest town. It was our city's first charity. It would not be the last.

By the end of the Civil War, Columbus had a wide variety of private charitable organizations dealing with a host of issues from public education to communicable disease prevention. But care for the elderly was not one of those concerns.

The reason for this was quite simple. The elderly, as we understand the term today, did not exist. There were several reasons for this state of affairs. First and foremost, there simply were not that many old people. The combination of hard living, predatory diseases and a world of smoke-filled air, contaminated water, and unrefrigerated food killed off many people before they reached the age of 50.

For the few people who survived all of this, families or friends were available to take care of the elderly.

But shortly after the Civil War, our technology began to save us from ourselves. The coming of water purification, sewage treatment, and improving standards of food preparation suddenly began to permit people to live longer. And so they did.

By the early 1880s, cities like Columbus suddenly found that a significant number of reasonably well educated and socially prominent widows and widowers of advanced age were in the interesting position of still being very much alive. These were certainly not persons one should or could send to the poorhouse.

So what to do? To Mrs. William Monypeny, the wife of a prominent businessman, the answer was obvious—build a home for these people. And in answer to the question of where to find the money to do so, Mrs. Monypeny had a novel solution. Hold a formal ball that would be the social event of the season and donate all of the proceeds to alleviating the problems of the "Proper but Poor" of Columbus.

So in December, 1886, Columbus held its first charity ball. It was a grand and glorious success and thousands of dollars were pledged to building a permanent home for the elderly in Columbus. Mr. William Monypeny donated the land, and in 1888, the Columbus Home for the Aged was constructed.

Originally built only for widows, the Home soon began to admit men as well. Governed by a private board, the Columbus Home for the Aged became one of the favorite private charities of Columbus.

And, most importantly, within a very few years the Home was admitting people regardless of their background.

Over the years, the Home was expanded on several occasions and ultimately several dozen people were living in the wonderful old building. In the early days, the Home was some distance out in the country and produced most of its own food. Even after Columbus grew out to meet the Home, the institution still produced most of its own produce and had one of the great private gardens of Columbus.

The Columbus Home for the Aged soon had its imitators but really had no equal until well into the 20th century.

Eventually, the combination of maintaining the aging building and meeting the needs of its people began to tell. By the late 1970s, the great building had been emptied and the last residents had been moved to other locations. For a time, the future of the Home was uncertain. But in the 1980s, the building was tastefully renovated and occupied by the architectural firm of Moody Nolan Ltd.

As we begin the 21st century, one of the major challenges we will face as a people is the continuing and relentless aging of America. The people who came to be called the post-World War II "baby-boomers" are now in their 50s. Within a few decades we will face on an even grander scale the prospect of large numbers of elderly people without homes or hope.

As it was a hundred years ago, we will be once again tested as a people when we respond to this need. Let us hope that we do as well in the future as we did in the past, with places like the Columbus Home for the Aged.

Born Brewery, c. 1900.
Courtesy of the Columbus Metropolitan Library.

29

Bier Hier!

As long as there has been a Columbus, people have been brewing up one thing or another to quench one's thirst and mellow one's mood at the same time. The early settlers seemed to have preferred distilled whiskey derived from the various grains and corn being grown in the area. Most of these concoctions were rather strong in both taste and combustibility. It is probably one measure of how much we have changed as a people that few of us today would even care to sip what some of our forebears once drank in almost unbelievable quantities.

Now this is not to suggest that everyone living on the frontier was a candidate for a substance abuse clinic. In fact most people only indulged themselves moderately if at all, and some towns like Granville or Westerville were totally "dry" at a relatively early point.

But Columbus originally was brought into being to be the capital city. The primary businesses in the early days were the restaurants, saloons and hostelries that served the government and the people who served the public servants.

Beginning in the 1830s, a continuous wave of German and Irish immigration totally transformed Columbus. The Germans did not look at their new world in quite the same way as many of the other people living in Columbus and central Ohio. As just one example among others, they did not look at beer in the same way many of the earlier settlers viewed the beverage.

Basically, beer was seen as a common part of everyday life. Beer was consumed with meals by whole families. Children were often weaned to beer rather than milk. And even the family pets were often given beer rather than water. There were some good reasons to do this. In an era of unpasteurized milk, beer was often safer than dairy products. And it was certainly safer than most of the disease-ridden water which filled the rivers and wells of central Ohio.

More importantly, beer became the beverage which welded German families together socially in the face of an often hostile outside world through a variety of institutions, including the famous "bier gartens" which flourished through most of the south end.

For most of the 1800s beer was part of the "definition" of the German community. And the people who brewed it were some of the most well-respected people in the city. Does this mean that Germans drank more alcohol in general and beer in particular than the other people of Columbus? No, not at all. But the German community defended its right to do so more vociferously than most.

Brewing beer was a family business in Columbus. The breweries were small and the quantities produced were limited to the amount which could be consumed locally. By the Civil War, several local families including the Schlees, Borns, and Hosters had come to dominate the local brewing business. And as similar businesses attract each other, the major breweries were located on Front Street just south of downtown, where they would stay for the next two generations. But brewing beer was just one of many things that people in the German community did with their lives.

When Conrad Born, Sr., died, he was not remembered primarily at the time as one of the three biggest brewers in Columbus. Rather he was recalled as the oldest butcher still practicing his craft in the city. In fact, most of the early brewers considered the production of beer to be just one of many things they did to make a living in the new city of Columbus.

This changed when the second and third generations of

the brewing families came into the business. Responding to the growing ease of transportation by railroad and the increasingly economical use of refrigeration, brewer after brewer began to sell his product on a regional rather than local basis. Ultimately, this led to the closing of many smaller breweries or their merger with larger local or regional producers. By 1900, this movement to unify in the face of competition had affected Columbus as well, and the Columbus Consolidated Brewing Company had come into being as a major regional competitor.

But a series of crippling strikes and the coming of the "wonderful experiment" of Prohibition ended all of that. Several of the breweries tried to make the transition to the manufacture of other products. But the buildings and equipment were old and the workers were really more highly skilled artisans than an industrial workforce. By the end of Prohibition in the 1930s, only a small remnant of the original brewing business survived. And by that time most of the German community which had provided the market for the product had either assimilated, acculturated, or simply moved on to different lifestyles.

With the passing of the brewing companies, the great brewery buildings became warehouses and wholesale centers. By the 1950s, Brewery Row seemed to be as threatened with demolition as the old German residential area nearby. But with the revival of German Village, the breweries were given a reprieve—and recent efforts at renovation have resulted in a newly revitalized Brewery District commercial area south of the downtown.

Today the Brewery District is not only a vibrant business district but a living reminder of the way of life of many of our people not so long ago.

Schiller Park.
Photo courtesy of Ed Lentz.

~30~
Schiller Park

Our city has had a significant German population for most of its history. True, the initial settlement of the area was by Virginians coming up the Scioto River valley and Yankees drifting south from the Western Reserve of Connecticut in what is now Northeast Ohio. But even in the early days, a trickle of German settlers had come to settle on the "High Banks opposite Franklinton at the Forks of the Scioto known as Wolf's Ridge" and now called Columbus.

That trickle became a flood as people from across a war-ravaged and economically devastated Europe fled to America in the 1830s and 1840s. By 1850, almost half the population of Columbus was German and most of those folks were living below Livingston Avenue in an area then called the Old South End. Today, we call it German Village.

It is easy to imagine that the Germans must have had a pathological fear of open space. Most of the houses in German Village seem to be almost shoehorned in place one next to the other. Actually this was not the case. The Germans loved fresh air and open spaces as much as most of us do.

The simple fact was that most of the German immigrants to Columbus were people of modest means who settled originally on the South End because the land was cheap. The land was cheap because the Scioto in those days was an open sewer for the city, and property below the town was therefore considerably cheaper than the land upriver. Housing was relatively inexpensive given the availability of local brick, but the combined cost of land and buildings added up. This meant that lots tended to be small and houses were constructed so that every inch of space was usable.

But even with small lots and modest scale, the homes themselves were built close to the street, leaving room in the backyard for a fenced-in lot and a bit of green space and garden. This was almost the reverse of the traditional settlement pattern in America's countryside. Used to open spaces, people in early American country homes tended to have large front porches which were well-used. In this way, the residents could see who was coming long before they got there. In a land where the Indian Wars raged in the living memory of many settlers, this was a distinct advantage.

Town houses in Columbus originally had front yards as well. But as noise, congestion, and hundreds of horses (and what horses leave behind) began to fill the streets, the logic of the German approach to backyard living began to make more sense. The Germans loved outdoor living. If not spending some time in one's own backyard, steady streams of people were always heading for the biergartens and outside restaurants which once outnumbered the churches in the South End of Columbus. But something else was lacking. German Village needed a park of its own.

Even the flood-prone residents of Old Franklinton across the river could use Sullivant's Prairie west of the village as a park. By the end of the Civil War, it seemed everyone had a park but the Germans.

Now the Germans did have Stewart's Grove. The 30-plus acres on the south side of German Village had been used for years for picnics and occasional public events. But it was private land, and its owners understandably liked to get paid for its use. Finally yielding to public pressure in 1867, City Council gave in and bought almost 25 acres for a park. The place was called City Park and City Park Street takes its name from this original title. Over the next 20 years as roads and landscaping were developed, a lake with a boathouse was added, and for a time a small zoo occupied a corner of the site. The most notable resident was an American eagle with an eight-foot wingspread.

Now it may surprise some of us that the people in German Village would pick a poet to be the "Person in the Park" instead of Bismarck, Frederick the Great, or even the legendary Hermann (who obliterated a few Roman legions in the Battle of Teutonburg Forest). In thinking that way, of course, we are only revealing our own view of the Germans, which have been shaped by two World Wars in this century.

In the 19th Century, most Germans were not Prussian autocrats nor even that militaristic. In fact, Germany as we understand it today did not even exist until late in the 1800s. Germans were linked by language and culture but not by nationalism until quite late in the 19th Century. For this reason, the heroes of the romantic revival in the mid-1800s tended to be writers, musicians, artists and poets. And among these, Friederich Schiller was considered by many to be the best.

So on July 4, 1889, ground was broken to prepare a place for the installation of a monument to Schiller. On July 4, 1891, a lifesize bronze statue of the poet was unveiled on the site with suitable pomp and bombast. And from that point on, the park has been Schiller Park. Over the years, the neighborhood went through enormous changes as the German population assimilated and left for the suburbs and new people moved in. Just when the district seemed to be in danger of demolition, a grass-roots movement sprang up, leading to one of the largest renovation projects in America—the German Village preservation area.

There are not many Germans left in German Village today. But the German heritage of Columbus lives on—in the streets, in the structures, and in the gaze of Schiller of Schiller Park.

Striking streetcar workers of 1890.
Courtesy of the Columbus Metropolitan Library.

~31~
The Streetcar Strike of 1890

The Columbus streetcar strike of 1890 was a cry of anguish and a warning. The cry was heeded. The warning was not. And when the cry came again, it would be an angry one indeed.

It all began innocently enough. Columbus, Ohio, was not what one would call a particularly pro-labor town in the 19th century. It was true that the American Federation of Labor and the United Mineworkers of America had held their organizing conventions in the capital city. But one could make the case that these meetings were held here more because of the city's central location and good rail service than because of the labor sentiments in the town. There had been occasional violent confrontations between working people and their employers at various times, especially during the 1877 railroad strike. But generally speaking, Columbus was not considered to be a hotbed of labor strife.

There were several reasons for this. Columbus had seen large scale immigration in the 1840s and 1850s, but the great waves of later immigration were missing the city. The reason was rather simple. Columbus had then what it has today—a well-diversified economy. While a large number of people toiled in factories, an even larger portion of the population worked for government or in what we today would call service industries. This mixture of varied work and a relatively well-assimilated population made the town a bit more stable—some would say stodgy—in comparison with the great cities of the East and lakefront Midwest.

By the late 1880s, Columbus was a thriving midwestern capital city whose population was rapidly approaching the 100,000 mark. It was a city of pleasant neighborhoods of well-built homes along tree-lined streets, and of impressive facilities like The Ohio State University and institutions to aid the blind, deaf, mentally ill, and developmentally disabled. It was also a city of occasional slums, a river that more closely resembled an open sewer, and a sky that was almost perpetually black from the coal smoke that provided heat, light, and power to the growing metropolis. In short it was a 19th Century American city with not a few problems but some decidedly bright prospects as well.

And linking all of the pieces of this urban puzzle together was the streetcar system. Begun in 1863 with a simple line up High Street, the streetcar system of Columbus had evolved into a huge enterprise of many different companies linking all parts of the city one with another. In less than 20 years, Columbus had become a streetcar city with the horse-drawn cars linking the streetcar suburbs surrounding the town to the vital business district in the center.

And making all of this happen was a group of hard-working men who worked extraordinarily long hours for very low pay. In 1890, union organizers convinced a number of the workers that the answer to improving their condition lay in organizing a union and using the strength of their numbers to force concessions from management. But management had problems of its own. The streetcar business had enormous investments in cars, tracks, barns, and horses as well as in its workers. Its profit margins were slim and it was not easy to find a way to meet the demands of the workers.

So in frustration, the members of the streetcar workers union met at midnight on June 3, 1890, at a local hall and voted to go on strike. In order to avoid a confrontation, the company did not run its cars on June 4. But on June 5, a single car ran several blocks as a test until it came to the intersection of Long and High Streets. Here the car ran into a mass of milling men who were not very happy to see the car on the city's streets. The terrified driver abandoned the car.

Striking workers removed the horses and led them to safety. They then turned the car sideways across the tracks and held an impromptu demonstration.

Over the next few days, the streetcar company obtained court injunctions to stop the interruption of its service. The union countered by quickly boarding a car as soon as it left its carbarn and, in the words of one account, subjected "the new crews to such annoyances as to make it impossible for them to proceed." More importantly, there were large crowds of people along the sidewalk shouting their support to the workers.

On June 9, the company reached an agreement with the workers which permitted an end to the strike. The major points of the agreement included a reduction of the day's work from 16 hours to twelve and a significant raise in pay. Both sides celebrated the end of the strike by running flag-bedecked cars through the city on the morning of June 10. No one had been seriously injured, nor had property been heavily damaged, and the strike had concluded in less than a week.

In July of 1910, the situation would be much different. Union and management were each unwilling to compromise and prepared for a long battle. They got one. Throughout the spring and summer of 1910, a virtual war raged between strikers and the streetcar company, with cars dynamited and the National Guard called in more than once to restore order. It was one of the longest periods of continuous civil strife in the city's history. The lessons of determination and settlement from the 1890 strike were set aside and a terrible time became a tragic one as well.

Crystal Ice Manufacturing Comanpy, c. 1900.
Courtesy of the Columbus Metropolitan Library.

~32~
The Crystal Ice Company

Looking at old photographs of the people and places of Columbus of many years ago, it is not too difficult to look beyond differences in dress and hair styles and see people like ourselves. But in many ways, the lifestyle of the people of Columbus was quite different than ours. To understand how life was fundamentally different in those days, one needs to understand how people of the time coped with one of the oldest concerns of people on the planet—the necessity of making things stay cold. It is somewhat ironic that people who had often had to struggle to stay warm in drafty, poorly heated homes had to also deal with how to keep things cold as well.

Today we take the easy and inexpensive availability of cold storage for granted. If we need a cold drink, we open the refrigerator and get one. In fact on many modern refrigerators, we do not even have to open the door—using instead a built in spigot on the outside of the machine. And we can buy food infrequently—once a week or once a month—and use it as we need it.

Not so very long ago, it was not so easy to keep things cold. Many persons who are still living can recall the time when refrigerators were unavailable and the most up-to-date device in the kitchen was a large wooden cabinet with two compartments—one on the top for food and the other on the bottom for ice. This was the golden age of the icebox.

Today the icebox seems like something of a rather inefficient way to keep things cold. The large block of melting ice kept food cool but certainly not cold and it ultimately led to a very heavy pan full of water that needed emptying. But in its time, the icebox was considered something of a luxury. Most people simply ate food in season and "put-up" as much food as possible by canning fruits and vegetables and smoking or drying meat for use during the long winters of the American Midwest.

In the winter, ice was cut from frozen rivers and ponds with long saws and stored in insulated pits or buildings for use at a later date. But like the springhouse or cellar, this was not a very efficient way to keep things cold.

As the Industrial Revolution transformed America, millions of people moved into cities to work in the factories and shops that were making this one of the richest countries in history. And the people living in cities needed to keep things cool as well. With the pollution of the rivers which often had previously provided ice, an alternative approach to inexpensive ice production was needed. Enter companies like the Crystal Ice Manufacturing Co. It was not the only artificial ice company in Columbus, but in the late 1890s it was one of the most successful.

Here is how ice was made in those days: "The water used is pumped from five artesian wells. . . . It is first boiled in huge tanks and converted to steam. This steam is passed through a series of pipes surrounded by cold water which speedily converts the steam back into water and causes it to deposit all lime, magnesia, sulphur, iron and similar foreign substances it may contain. It then goes through a filter of charcoal and sponges and after purifying, it is ready for freezing.

"It is run into zinc cans of the capacity of blocks of ice and is there frozen in 48 hours by chemical action taking place outside the cans as follows: The can is placed in a vat of salt water reaching almost to its top, but not high enough to run over into the pure water contained in the can. Running through this salt water surrounding the can are a number of small pipes containing ammonia and another anti-hydrate gas, which have a tendency to absorb the heat from the salt water and reduce it to a temperature of 10 degrees above zero....When the freezing process is completed, the can is drawn from the vat and sprinkled with warm water which loosens it from its can. The ice block is run down an incline to a storage room, ready for delivery."

Using a similar technology, the company also operated a cold storage warehouse at its facility at 397 West Broad Street. The facility could hold more than 55,000 barrels of fruits, meats, eggs and seafood for local stores and restaurants, while the ice making plant could produce more than 120 tons of ice a day to meet commercial and residential needs

Companies like Crystal Ice changed the way people ate in central Ohio. No longer did even working class people have to rely on foods only procurable in season. With readily available, inexpensive ice, most of the people in America's cities could shop less often and enjoy more and different sorts of food.

But when a new technology, the modern refrigerator, came on the scene in the 1910s, a population well accustomed to the availability of conveniently cooled food was already on hand. The convenience and relative inexpensiveness of the refrigerator led to the eventual transformation of the domestic ice business to its present form of providing ice for special needs and uses.

In many houses built a century or more ago, one can still find a strange pass-through on the outside wall of the kitchen. Lined with zinc, the passage usually forms an 18" cube. It is the ice door. Leaving his wagon or truck at the street, the ice man would carry a block of ice up to the house with a large pair of metal tongs while resting the ice on a hip covered with a thick leather apron.

Like the bread man and the milk man, the ice man does not come by any more. To many people living in suburban symbols of success who daily wait for the mail and the human contact it brings, perhaps the passing of the ice man is marked with as much pathos as progress.

The Hallwood Block Company, c. 1892.
Courtesy of the Columbus Metropolitan Library.

33

Henry S. Hallwood

Henry Hallwood was born near Warrington in Lancashire, England, in 1848. He was the son of sea captain who had a rather interesting career in his own right. Rising rapidly as a commercial seafarer, Hallwood's father was a captain at the age of 19. While hunting seals in the far north, Captain Hallwood was separated from his ship and spent three days floating alone on an ice floe. When he was found by his crew, he was frozen to the ice and apparently dead. But a quick-witted seaman rubbed Hallwood with snow and slowly fed him stimulants until he came around.

Perhaps because of this close brush with death, Captain Hallwood left the life of the sea and opened a commercial business in Warrington. Eventually his son joined him in that business under the name of Hallwood and Son. And such might have been the beginning of a quiet life in small town England except for the intervention of romance. In 1874, young Henry Hallwood fell in love with Annie Lockey and eloped with her. The only problem was that the lovely Miss Lockey was only 16 and the marriage was not looked upon with favor by the young girl's parents.

The couple fled to America, where they stayed for a time until a return to England led to a reconciliation with the bride's family. Liking what he found in America, Hallwood returned to the United States and settled in West Virginia with his wife and the first of what would eventually be a family of eight children.

Hallwood entered the mining business to support his growing family but could not make a success of it. By the mid-1880s, he arrived in Columbus looking for something new. He found his niche first in the construction business building sewer lines and other public works for the rapidly growing city. But he made his fortune in paving bricks.

Most streets in most cities in post-Civil War America were

dirt road or gravel paths. Only the most heavily traveled roads had any kind of paving at all. Various kinds of paving had been tried over the years—from cobblestones to wooden blocks. But most methods of street paving were either quite expensive or not very effective. The continuing growth of traffic on the streets called for some kind of solution to this problem. Eventually the solution was found in a hard and durable brick product called a paving block.

The success of the paving block meant that the streets of America's cities became brick streets. There were dozens of producers of paving blocks, each of whom imprinted his name onto each block as a sort of early form of individualized advertising. One name that people saw quite frequently was 'Hallwood.' By the early 1890s the Ohio Paving Company was producing 350,000 paving blocks a day in twelve plants across the Midwest. The plants were located in the heart of Ohio's clay country in the area between Portsmouth on the south, Zanesville on the east, and Columbus on the west. The Hallwood block was used in places as far-removed as Saginaw, Michigan, in the north to Chattanooga in the south, and as far east as Hartford and Baltimore.

At this point, as middle age approached, Henry Hallwood might have been expected by some to simply continue to build his successful business and take well-deserved pride in his accomplishments. But people who expected Henry Hallwood to slow down did not know Henry Hallwood. By the mid-1890s, Hallwood realized that the people who made their money in transportation were making their fortune the way it had been made a generation before. The new money, the new fortunes, were going to be in manufacturing—the making of machines to help people do their work more easily.

Hallwood acquired the patents to just such a machine—a cash register—and set out manufacturing them in large numbers. At the turn of the century, there were literally dozens of manufacturers of cash registers. But most of these companies either never got off the ground at all, or made little progress until they were bought out or fought out by one of the larger concerns. The master of this no-holds-barred competition was a business man from Dayton named John H. Patterson. His National Cash Register Company made many of its own rules in its relentless march to market dominance. Few companies could stand in the way of "The Cash." Few ever tried. The Hallwood Cash Register Company not only tried, it gave NCR some rather stiff competition indeed.

By the early 1900s the only way that Patterson and National Cash could finally find to eliminate Hallwood was to buy up his machines and then resell them at a cheaper price. In short, Patterson's idea was to keep Hallwood's machines off the market by buying many of them himself. The plan worked. In a few years, Hallwood was forced to close his business. But he retained his patents and later licensed them to the American Cash Register Company.

By this time, National Cash Register controlled 95% of the cash register market. It was at this point that Hallwood and American Cash Register launched their final assault on National Cash Register. At the complaint of American Cash Register and others, the federal government brought suit in anti-trust against Patterson and his company. Over several years and more than 2,000 pages of testimony, the government showed how Patterson had dominated his market and suppressed his competition. By 1913, Patterson and NCR were facing penalties, which were only avoided by a negotiated settlement with the government that resulted in a consent agreement lay-ing out the limits of competition in the cash register business.

Today there is no statue of Henry Hallwood in Columbus. But if one wants to find a token of him, all that one needs to do is walk the brick byways of the inner city and look down. And there in the streets he made, the name of Hallwood is with us still.

The Columbus Buggy Company, c. 1888.
Courtesy of the Columbus Metropolitan Library.

34

The Columbus Buggy Company

There was a time when Columbus, Ohio, was one of America's great manufacturing centers. Just a century ago, Columbus was the Buggy Capital of the World. And the Columbus Buggy Company was the biggest and most successful of the 22 buggy companies in the city. How this all came to pass and how it ended is one of the better stories worth retelling in the history of our city.

Making leather from animal skins is a tough, dirty, and extremely smelly business which is not for those with faint hearts or tender digestions. For that reason Tunis Peters and a few other tanners had the creek on the south end pretty much to themselves and it was not too long before it came to be called Peters Run.

George M. Peters, Tunis's grandson, went to work at the age of 16 to help support his family. He decided to get into a business that had more chance of success than tanning or trunk making, but which could still use his leather-working skills. He went into buggy making in 1856. Buggies in those days were essentially products of small groups of individual craftsmen who molded wood, metal, and leather into literally moveable works of art. Because the work was slow, meticulous and detailed, buggies tended to be expensive and only affordable by the well-off.

George Peters developed a reputation as one of the best buggy detail painters in the business and his partnership with the Benns Brothers, William and John, was quite successful. But George Peters had other plans. He felt that buggies could be made much more cheaply for more people. This was possible if only certain limited styles were made from largely interchangeable parts which were manufactured by steam-powered machines rather than by men with hand tools.

He finally persuaded his partners to let him experiment

with this idea. In 1865, he contracted with a prison labor contractor to have the parts for 100 buggies produced at the old Ohio Penitentiary. He then employed people to assemble the buggies and sold them at half the price of comparable vehicles.

George Peters wanted to continue with this sort of production, but the Benns brothers would have none of it. They were rather fond of the old ways of doing things. So George entered into a new partnership with his younger brother Oscar and an acquaintance named Clinton D. Firestone.

C.D. Firestone was a Canton, Ohio, native who had done all sorts of things since leaving home to join the Union Army at the age of 16. Firestone had brains, talent, and a lot of marketing and financial experience. He also had $5000 in available cash.

The new company began as the Iron Buggy Company in 1875 at the corner of High Street and Hickory Alley, making an all metal vehicle. The partners branched out into the leather dashboard business and the Peters Dash Company soon was making more money than the buggy business.

But George Peters still believed that a properly organized factory not only could make buggies more cheaply—they could also make them more profitably than anyone had ever done. He had convinced his partners of this simple point and in 1878 they set out to prove it to a waiting world.

They were at the right place at the right time. The Hocking Valley Railroad had opened up southeast Ohio to exploitation of the huge iron, coal and wood resources of that region. Huge amounts of these materials were now available very cheaply to people who knew what to do with them.

The Columbus Buggy Company knew what to do with them. They used their experience with division of labor and specialization of production of interchangeable parts to assemble buggies in a continuous systematic way by relatively unskilled labor. The Columbus Buggy Company did not invent the assembly line. But they made it into what we know it to be today. The Company had its principal factory on the near northwest side of the city near the railyards. From that location they produced more buggies more quickly and more cheaply than anyone had ever done before. By the early 1890s, the factory was making more than 100 buggies a day and was employing more than 1,200 people—or one in every 20 workers in the city of Columbus. The Peters and Firestone families were among the city's social elite. In 1895, a young man visited the Columbus factory to see if the rubber tires used on some carriages might be adaptable to his experimental motor-car. His name was Henry Ford and he learned quite a bit. Eventually Ford would work closely with Clinton Firestone's cousin Harvey, who had also learned a lot about mass production by working for Columbus Buggy before going into the rubber tire business on his own.

The devastating depression of the 1890s followed a disastrous fire in 1886. For a time things did not look good, and in a nightmare of depression, Oscar Peters took his own life. But George Peters and Clinton Firestone refused to be defeated. They reorganized the company and began building motor cars as well as buggies in a new factory to the east of the Ohio Penitentiary.

For a time it too was successful. But the disastrous flood of 1913 inundated the factory and virtually destroyed the business with the buildings. Today there is very little tangibly left of the Columbus Buggy Company in Columbus.

But visit any factory anywhere in the world and you will find people still using the lessons of division of labor, specialization of assembly and an insistence on quality in all aspects of production that made the company a legend in American manufacturing. In that sense, the real legacy of the Columbus Buggy Company is very much alive and with us.

Dr. Samuel Hartman, c. 1909.
Courtesy of the Columbus Metropolitan Library.

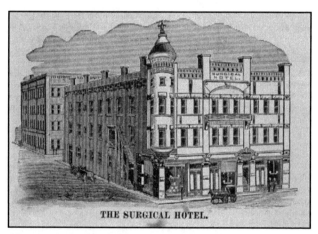

Hartman's Surgical Hotel, c. 1900.
Courtesy of the Columbus Metropolitan Library.

A Palliative Called Peruna

Early in 1882, one of the more fascinating people in the history of our city arrived in Columbus. Dr. Samuel Brubaker Hartman (known as SB to friend and foe alike) was actually a quite competent orthopedic surgeon for most of his career. But in Columbus, he heard the call of Chief Peruna.

Hartman had been born in Lancaster County, Pennsylvania, in 1830. After a relatively uneventful childhood he had ended up rather mysteriously in Cincinnati in 1845 at a place called Farmer's College, where he completed the VERY rough equivalent of a high school education. Shortly thereafter, he entered into medical apprenticeship with one Dr. Shackelford of Medway, Ohio (then as now a small village near Dayton). By 1857, he had completed medical studies in Cleveland and New York and was in practice in Lancaster, Pennsylvania, back where he had started. Dr. Hartman married in 1859 and, by all accounts, made a nice living as a physician and manufacturer of "medical devices" for a number of years.

In 1882, for reasons that are not entirely clear, Dr. Hartman came to Columbus. He established a quite successful medical practice which centered near the intersection of Fourth and Main Streets in downtown Columbus. The building in the picture is the third place to be used as a Hotel and sits near the same site where the first two had been. It was built in 1902.

Medicine was a little more rough and ready a century ago. Doctors and hospitals often were viewed, with good reason, as places to visit only when one was at death's door. Dr. Hartman's facility, just up the street from the hotel, was much different. It was clean, well-equipped and staffed with bright, capable people. People actually left this hospital in better, or at least no worse, shape than when they entered.

Hartman was enormously successful. People were

obliged to make reservations for admittance months in advance in an era when most persons would not enter a hospital at all. This is not to say that we would agree today with everything that Dr. Hartman prescribed. He at least had the virtue of being usually right, if occasionally for the wrong reasons. Many of his peers were wrong for the wrong reasons. In any case, the good doctor was able to expand his practice, build a nice home, and generally succeed in his chosen field.

Then one night he had a dream. The ghost of a long-dead Native American named Chief Peruna appeared to Dr. Hartman and confidently explained the real cause of what ailed most of mankind, and what could be done about it. Almost every disease imaginable was actually a variation on catarrh (congestion). Heart disease was due to catarrh of the heart. Cancerous tumors were due to catarrh in the affected organ. Strokes were the result of catarrh of the brain. And so on...

Fortunately a cure was at hand, in the form of an ancient formula handed down through Chief Peruna's family for many years. In an act of eleemosynary goodwill, the Chief revealed this secret formula to Dr. Hartman so that he could share it with a waiting world. In return, Dr. Hartman named the elixir Peruna.

At first, Peruna did not sell too well. Part of this was due to the fact that it had a terrible taste. Part of this was also due to the fact that Dr. Hartman had little marketing sense at all. This all changed when Dr. Hartman received an order for two train cars full of the tonic from a young man in El Paso, Texas. Dr. Hartman wanted to meet anyone who could sell this much of his elixir.

The young man was Frederick Schumacher. Mr. Schumacher was not a doctor, nor a pharmacist, nor even a chemist. He was a salesman. In short order, young Mr. Schumacher moved to leadership in the company, married the boss's daughter, and changed the way consumer products were marketed in America. Schumacher did not invent the testimonial message, the free sample, or the concept of repetitive

advertising. But he took these and many other approaches and created a comprehensive marketing strategy virtually without precedent in America. Using these techniques, He made a fortune for himself and Dr. Hartman.

Using the profits of Peruna, Dr. Hartman built a factory and bottling plant in downtown Columbus near his hospital, built a magnificent theater on Statehouse Square, and linked all of this with his own private railroad to the Hartman Farms south of the city. At one time the Farms were the largest agricultural complex east of the Mississippi. It seemed for a time that nothing could impede the progress of Peruna.

In 1906, the passage of the Pure Food and Drug Act stopped Peruna in its tracks. A report on the product declared that Peruna consisted mostly of alcohol with some flavoring. Regulators demanded that the Doctor should, in the words of a reporter from that time, "either change his formula or open a saloon!"

Reluctantly, Dr. Hartman changed the formula. Remarkably the elixir continued to sell quite briskly until the late 1920s, long after the death of Dr. Hartman. Dr. Hartman's heirs ultimately closed the business and the bottling plant, and placed most of the farm land into a bank administered trust. Most of them have since moved away from Columbus. Frederick Schumacher, a patron of the arts, gave much of his fortune to establish and maintain what is now the Columbus Museum of Art.

The interesting thing about all of this is that to most people across the country, Dr. Hartman is usually remembered as one of the classic snake-oil salesmen of his time. But in Columbus, there are still people living who can remember the Doctor, his hospital, his gifts to cultural and social groups, and most of all his commitment to healing and relieving of pain. In short, he was a good man who did good work. And Peruna? Well, even the best of people have their eccentricities!

Automobilists in Franklin Park, c. 1910.
Courtesy of the Columbus Metropolitan Library.

36

The Automobilists

It was over a century ago that the first automobile appeared on the streets of Columbus, to the awe and amusement of most people and the consternation of most nearby horses. It was a Winton and was ably driven by its owner Mr. Campbell Chittenden. The Chittendens were best known at the time for the now-vanished hotel that bore their name and for which Chittenden Avenue near The Ohio State University is one of the few reminders of their former influence. The car itself still survives and is prominently displayed among the exhibits at the Ohio Historical Center.

Let's return to that simpler time of a century ago and find out what a few of the "best people" of Columbus thought about their new "motor cars."

As Spring approached, Mrs. Theodore Lindenberg departed for New York with her husband in their touring car. Larger than their "town car," the touring car was built to endure the unpaved roads which constituted most of America's highways. Before she left, she shared her opinions of this new kind of transportation with a reporter for a local paper.

"How does it seem to be the controlling power in an automobile? It is a sensation that has about all of the pleasurable excitement of a swift ride in a trolley car with the added satisfaction that comes with the power to control this motion to the second in speed, and to the inch in direction, so that one may turn or stop at will, and combined with this satisfaction is anticipation, for one is never quite sure that there may be a stop that is not desired."

"Then it has the fascination of the unknown?"

"Yes, for the little element of danger makes it doubly

desirable. In fact it is difficult to express just how one feels when driving a motor, for it is a combination of everything that is delightful. One returns from a drive vitalized in proportion to the speed. Although I am sincerely opposed to the reckless driving that endangers others, I like to feel the puff of the vibrations that send me over the road at a swift pace, bringing the exhilaration that is free of the fatigue that follows so many other forms of pleasure."

"You anticipate much pleasure from your coming trip, then?"

"Very much. It is so pleasant to drive through the country in a motor car. It is the very refinement of travel, combining privacy with speed."

Another convert to Age of the Motor Car was Henry Neil, a descendant of the legendary William Neil, the Stagecoach King. Then President of the Automobile Club, Mr. Neil was wont to hold forth from the porch of his fashionable suburban home, Indianola, at the intersection of Fifteenth and Indianola Avenues, on subjects of interest. One of those subjects was motor cars.

"Motor driving is superb. There is nothing like it. I am passionately fond of horses, but I prefer the automobile as a means of transit for a number of reasons. One is that no matter how cold or warm it may be, one may use it without the hesitation that always comes when one has to risk exposing horses to inclement weather. But even conceding their superiority for speed and use, do you think they will ever quite take the place of horses? I mean in the affections. It seems infinitely sad to think of the passing of the horse."

It was noted that a slight shadow crossed Mr. Neil's face as he began his response. "This is the saddest thing connected with what one may term the rise of the automobile; nevertheless I believe in time the motors will wholly supplant the animal we

142

have loved so, for one comes to feel that these vehicles are part of oneself through their responsiveness. They obey the slightest touch as though endowed with life and reason.

"There is a another reason I think motors are destined to be the favorite vehicle. One may go through the country, visiting out of the way places where railway trains never penetrate, and it would be impossible to take a horse to remain any length of time, without so much trouble that the pleasure would be materially reduced. I drove 4,000 miles last summer and 5,000 this summer. I don't care much for riding in town, for the streets are so miserable, but I enjoy a long drive over good roads.

"I am pleased to see how rapidly they are gaining in popular favor. I measure this popularity by the increasing number of machines. A year ago there were not more than 30 motors in Columbus. Today there are not less than 150 and the demand is so great that the factories cannot supply it."

We conclude with a few comments from Miss Maud Huston about her motor car. Speaking almost a century ago, her concerns are contemporary to her time but common to our own as well. At the time she made these remarks, she "was the only woman in town who operated a steam powered car."

"No I do not feel the slightest fear in driving my motor. In fact I feel safer than I do behind a horse, because I know I can control the automobile, and one is never too sure of a horse. This simply means that I have more confidence in myself than I have in any animal, however intelligent. I have been trained to manage the motor, and if you trust yourself with me, I shall be pleased to let you know as a personal experience, how it seems to ride in an automobile, just as soon as mine, which is undergoing repairs, is returned."

The current home of The Columbus Urban League.
Photo ourtesy of Ed Lentz.

~37~
The Columbus Urban League

The Columbus Urban League celebrated its 80th anniversary in 1998. This is a wonderful achievement for any organization, and an especially notable one for a group which has had to struggle more than once for its very existence. The League has changed with the times to be sure, but it has been strikingly dedicated as well to the goals it established many years ago.

The National Urban League was founded in 1910 and soon established its headquarters in New York City. America at this time was a highly segregated society in both the North and the South. The "Jim Crow" laws of the post-Reconstruction South were more blatant and repressive, but northern society also imposed a strict division of the races. And while most black schools, restrooms, and other public accommodations were supposed to be "separate but equal," they were not. In the words of one who lived through that period, "separate but awful was more like it!"

But the very industrial and urban revolution that made life in early 20th-Century America so difficult for virtually everyone except the well-to-do, was also the force which began to liberate black America as well. By the early 1900s, the great industrial cities of the East and Midwest were acting as melting pots not only for every imaginable ethnic group but for black America as well.

The great factories needed huge numbers of unskilled people to do the dangerous, dirty, and difficult work more experienced and educated people simply would not do. With the immense waves of immigrants from eastern and southern Europe sweeping into the cities came first a trickle and then a steady stream of poor people, black and white, from Appalachia and the deep South as well.

With the gathering of larger and larger numbers of black people in northern cities came a new awakening of social and political consciousness. In 1909, the National Association for the Advancement of Colored People was founded. Under the uncompromising editorship of W.E.B. DuBois, the NAACP newspaper, *The Crisis*, became a voice for change in American race relations.

But while many people agreed with the goals and activities of the NAACP, just as many or more found the group not particularly relevant to their immediate needs for jobs, education or economic security. It was to answer these needs that the National Urban League was brought into being. Conceived as an interracial partnership of blacks and whites to improve the lot of all people in general and blacks in particular, the League from the start was non-confrontational and problem-solving in orientation.

In 1910s Columbus, a group like this made a lot of sense. It was a growing capital city of moderate size and opinions. The black community was well established because of the long history of Columbus as a service city. And while Columbus had been a hot-bed of anti-slavery agitation before the Civil War and a major "switching station" on the Underground Railroad in the 1850s, all of those activities had happened a long time before.

The National Urban League had been in existence for seven years before it came to Columbus. Two factors sparked its coming. One was World War I. The other was a man named Nimrod Allen.

World War I sparked a sudden and rapid boom in industrial production to support the war effort. Every northern city with any factories at all suddenly needed more workers than could be found. From the rural south, the stream of people moving north became a flood. Among American blacks it was called the "Great Migration" and it doubled the black population of Columbus in less than a year.

Many of the people coming north had never lived in close quarters in a city before and had little idea how to cope. Many people didn't survive at all as poor housing, sanitation, and diet ravaged the new arrivals. In the midst of these problems, Nimrod Allen saw the Urban League as a way to help the black community in Columbus.

Born in the south, Allen had come north to be educated at Wilberforce University and the Yale Divinity School. In 1915, he came to Columbus to direct the segregated Spring

Street branch of the YMCA. In 1917, he brought together several concerned social service professionals to form the Federated Social and Industrial Movement for the Negro. In 1918, the "Federated" reconstituted itself as the Columbus chapter of the Urban League. Allen was its unpaid Secretary for several years while continuing to work at the YMCA. And in 1921, he left the YMCA and became the Director of the League. He would stay in that job for the next 33 years.

Nimrod Allen and the directors who followed him have had the help of hundreds of residents of Columbus, black and white, over the years. All of these people have shared a common goal—to improve the social and economic condition of the black community of the city. To do this the League has undertaken a wide variety of activities in employment training and placement, public education, and housing improvement. In addition the League has consistently worked to improve positive communication and contact among the races in Columbus.

At times, the League has been viewed as too activist by some. This was especially true during the boycotts of segregated grocery stores in the 1930s and through the long non-violent struggle for improved economic and social conditions in the 1950s and 1960s. At other times, when passions ran high and confrontations turned violent, the calming voice of the League was seen as a "sell-out" by more militant protestors. At one point, Nimrod Allen recalled being called a communist and a fascist in two different telephone calls only ten minutes apart. "But," he noted, "at least they keep calling."

Over the past 80-plus years, the Columbus Urban League has moved several times and had several Directors. These people have touched the lives of thousands of people and, despite several close calls with economic doom, have always managed to survive to serve another day. It is perhaps a quintessential example of a type of American institution that we probably need in greater numbers.

Chic Harley, c. 1916.
Courtesy of the Columbus Metropolitan Library.

~39~
Chic Harley

Believe it or not, there was a time not so long ago when watching college football was not something bordering on a secular religious experience for much of the population of Ohio's capital city.

In those simpler days between the turn of the century and the 1920s, football was just another interscholastic sport like hockey, track and wrestling. The truly awe-inspiring sport was baseball, which was a game of strategy as well as strength and intellect. Football on the other hand was a cleaned up and toned down version of its rather racy and rambunctious predecessor—rugby. As it was explained to me many years ago: "Football is Rugby for people who want to keep their teeth."

But both games were team struggles which relied less on grace and finesse and more on brute force and muscle. Or at least so it seemed.

Between 1910 and 1920, this commonly held image of the game began to change. Part of the reason for the change was the adoption of football as a fully recognized intercollegiate sport and its growing popularity among younger Americans. Partly too, the rules of the sport were evolving and the game began to become more open and less brutal than it once had been. And finally, football began to be popular because of the exploits of a small but growing number of truly remarkable players.

In Columbus, Ohio, between 1916 and 1920, one man virtually reinvented football for its fans and supporters at The Ohio State University. His name was Charles "Chic" Harley and he was a legend in his own time.

Born in Michigan, Chic Harley had ended up in Columbus with his family and attended East High School. By today's standards of big players with even bigger egos he was not all that much to look at. He was 5'7" tall and weighed in at 145 pounds. But on the football field he could do it all. He could run. He could kick. And he could outplay almost anybody on any team including his own. He was, in short, a wonder to behold. In the course of three years at East, his team only lost one game—his last one.

Recruited heavily by most of the major football colleges in the country, Harley decided to stay in Columbus and attend Ohio State. He had made up his mind while still in high school that he wanted to play for the new coach at OSU, John Wilce, and see if he could help the struggling football program in Columbus. But first he had to help himself. Chic Harley was probably one of the greatest all-around athletes in Ohio State's history. There were few sports he could not play and play well. Unfortunately, he did not have the same natural talent with his academic work. Harley struggled with his studies all through college and often was in danger of losing his athletic eligibility. But with persistence and a lot of encouragement from his teammates and friends, he managed to stay in school.

Chic Harley played for the varsity football team at Ohio State for a total of three years between 1916 and 1919. He missed one year because of his service in World War I. In that time he established himself as one of the great players in any era in college football.

He not only was a great all-around athlete. He also had a natural sense of the drama of the game as well. Time after time, Ohio State would find itself in a close game only to see Harley punt, pass or run his way to victory.

It seemed at times that he was almost playing to the crowd. He would accept a kick-off and wait in the backfield while he sized up where the opposition was placing itself. Then at the last possible moment he would be off like a shot, scampering down the field for a major advance. And if anyone had the temerity to get in his way, he would more often than not simply knock them down. Chic Harley may have been small but he was tough—very tough.

By the time Chic Harley was done at Ohio State, the school had won two Big Ten titles and Harley was one of the few people before or since to be selected as an All-American for all three years of his varsity play. During his career, Ohio State had won 21 games, tied one, and only lost one. And again it was the last game of Chic Harley's last season. When that game ended an era ended as well.

It was at the height of Harley's fame that a serious move began to build a new football stadium to replace old and outdated Ohio Field. The fundraising was extraordinarily successful due to football's new popularity in central Ohio. And even though Chic Harley never played there, it is in a real sense the "House that Harley Built."

Chic Harley died in April 1974 in a Veterans Hospital in Danville, Illinois. He had not played football in decades but his passing was a major news story in Columbus. And that should not be surprising. Because over the years, college football became the sport of preference due to the efforts of dozens of young men who followed Chic Harley and the game he played so well.

People have often tried to compare Harley to the greats who followed him—people like Howard "Hopalong" Cassidy and Archie Griffin, the only two-time winner of the Heisman Trophy. It is not a fair comparison. Over the years, the game has changed and the players have changed with it.

The only fair judgment is to say that in their time and in their way each of these people, with their team mates, was the best that Ohio State produced. If you would find a monument to Chic Harley, come to Ohio Stadium in Columbus on a home football weekend and listen. In the roar of the crowd, you will hear his name. I know I can.

Greenlawn Abbey, where Thurston the magician is buried. Photo courtesy of Ed Lentz.

~40~
Thurston the Magician

It was called the "Wonder Show of the Universe." And what the title may have lacked in modesty, was more than made up for in the show itself. In the period between 1900 and the 1920s, there were "magic shows," "magicians," and "Masters of Sleight of Hand." And then there was Thurston. He was quite simply the best there was at what he did best. And what he did best was MAGIC.

This was a time when most people lived a little more simply than we live today, went to work and to bed with the sun, before the age of radio, movies and television. People were entertained by watching real people do all sorts of things—from theater, to concerts, to circuses. But in a real sense, the presentations our grandparents saw as children were not that much different than what we see today. People then and now liked to be thrilled, amused, and even frightened by the shows which came to town. And occasionally they enjoyed being totally, completely, and utterly enchanted by what appeared to be—but which everyone knew couldn't be—magic.

In this world of not so long ago, Howard Thurston enthralled a generation by doing things on stage which were patently impossible. He regularly sawed people in half and put them back together. He made large animals like elephants disappear right in front of your very eyes. He turned statues into living people. He made a girl levitate. And he regularly invited people on stage to see that what he was doing was "not a trick."

Of course, everyone knew it was trick. The whole question was, as it always has been with magicians, "How did he do that?"

Howard Thurston claimed in his press releases that it was the result of his being taught by Islamic mystics who kidnapped him at the age of three from Algiers, where his father was the American Consul. People loved hearing such things, but of course, like most of his show—it was a little hard to believe.

It was especially hard to believe if you happened to be living in Columbus, Ohio, in the 1870s and knew Howard Thurston to be the bright and, shall we say, "assertive" son of a local carriage maker. To make a little extra money, Howard's father made meat tenderizing mallets from scrap wood, and the boy began his career by selling the tools on downtown street corners. From there he branched out into newspaper sales and working as a bellhop in a local hotel.

Leaving school behind, Howard Thurston left Columbus to find a career that befitted his slight build and 5'5" height. He thought that future lay in following the horses and being one of the great jockeys of his time. By the time he was 20, he knew that his future lay elsewhere and he was on the streets of New York selling newspapers again.

Over the next few years he toyed with the idea of a career in the ministry, but ultimately decided to follow a decidedly more secular line of work. Fascinated with the work of magicians he had seen, he decided to become one himself. By the late 1880s he was touring the Midwest as a midway performer with the Sells Brothers Circus.

Thurston's big break came when he began to specialize in card tricks, developing some new ones of his own as he went along. His most famous illusion involved having the card mysteriously float from the deck to his hand with no apparent assistance. Touring Europe and Asia, Thurston became well-enough known that he was able to secure a place on the vaudeville circuit by the turn of the century.

A man of endless energy and enthusiasm, Thurston convinced the greatest magician of his age, Harry Keller, to name him as his heir. Keller died in 1908, and from that point on Thurston's future was made.

Thurston was the greatest magician of his day because he was relentless in his pursuit of an endlessly bigger and better show. And his audiences knew it. Before Thurston, most magic shows had four or five really eye-opening tricks. Thurston's basic show had 18. People waited in long lines for Thurston's shows, but as more than one observer noted—the best shows were worth the wait.

Before Thurston, magicians were essentially stage presenters and little more. Thurston dabbled in theater productions, radio drama, and magazine articles. His auto-biography, *My Life of Magic*, sold quite well indeed.

Through a long and eventful career, Thurston was married four times and made more than a million dollars from his magic. Unfortunately, he was not as good in judging his financial partners as he was in doing his magic. He lost most of his money through incredibly naive investments in Florida swamps, Canadian prairie, and complicated machines that sounded interesting but never worked.

On October 5, 1936, the 67 year-old magician finished a show in Charleston, West Virginia, and was leaving a local restaurant when he fell to the floor with a paralytic stroke. Over the next few months he fought to regain his health and talked of taking a new mystery play called "The Creeps" to Broadway.

It was not to be. On April 13, 1937, he died of a massive cerebral hemorrhage in Miami Beach. But Thurston was not the type to let a little thing like death end his career. He had told his wife that, no matter how difficult it might be, he would eventually return on the anniversary of his death, to any people assembled at his tomb. For many years thereafter, a small group of friends and relatives would gather at Thurston's grave in Columbus on each and every anniversary of his death and wait for him to come to them. So far he has not come.

Transcontinental Air Transport over downtown, c. 1929.
Courtesy of Ed Lentz.

~41~
Port Columbus Airport

People have dreamed of being able to fly like birds for as long as we have had legends and histories to tell us about them. But for most of human history, the only beings able to fly other than birds were the occasional deity and that rare person like Icarus who tried to fly for himself. And we all remember the misfortune he encountered.

For the first 30 years of its history, not much flew in Columbus except the birds, bullets, and balderdash one usually associates with life in a capital city on the moving frontier. But in 1842, the world changed when Richard Clayton arrived in town. Mr. Clayton was a self-proclaimed "aeronaut" who proposed to take his hydrogen-filled balloon from downtown Columbus to . . . well, to wherever the balloon wanted to go.

In this case, the balloon wanted to go to somewhere near Newark. Mr. Clayton later wrote of his adventures for a local paper, remarking on the peace and serenity of his flight. He also noted that the experience would have been exhilarating if he had not been deathly ill from a combination of air sickness and breathing a lot of the hydrogen that filled the balloon.

At least Mr. Clayton got back to the ground safely. A lot of his early aerial colleagues did not fare as well. But this did not keep a number of people from trying. Over the next several decades, balloon ascensions became a standard attraction of the fairs, carnivals and circuses that provided relief from the plagues, floods and endless labor that was the lot of many people living a century ago.

But that is all balloons really were—an entertainment and a diversion. A balloon ride might be the most exciting thing to arrive in Columbus since the Indian Wars. But no one was really contemplating moving large numbers of people or freight by air.

Even when the Wright Brothers successfully demonstrated in 1903 that one could fly without a bag of gas or hot air, most people were not too terribly impressed. Early aircraft were literally held together with glue and baling wire and were about as fragile as they looked. Even though "aeroplanes" were exciting to watch, most people were content to do just that and leaving the flying to others.

And over the years people found a lot to watch. In 1910, a man named Philip Parmalee threw a large roll of silk from a store in Dayton into his airplane and flew the cargo to Columbus. When the plane touched down in the old Driving Park race track, ending the first commercial cargo flight in history, a huge crowd was on hand to purchase little one inch squares of the cloth with an autographed postcard.

In the same year the intrepid Barney Oldfield claimed that his customized racing car could beat any airplane ever made. So a race was held between the car and a plane. Many people said it wasn't really a race so much as an exhibition. But in any case it was a lot of fun, even if most people continued to believe that flying would never amount to much. But in less than 20 years most people were proven wrong.

World War I changed most people's attitudes toward airplanes. The planes were light, fragile, and not very safe. But, mounted with heavy machine guns and bombs, they proved to be formidable and versatile killing machines. By the early 1920s, new designs of both the machines and their engines were making flying safer and more popular than ever. The great air races of the 1920s drew thousands of spectators and experiments with rigid dirigibles were proving that there was at least a modest market for passenger air travel.

But it would take something of a leap of faith to form a company to move both people and freight on a regular basis. The man who made that leap was Charles A. Lindbergh. And the place he made it from was Columbus, Ohio.

Lindbergh became the first man to fly the Atlantic alone

in 1927. Following up on the nearly hysterical adoration he received when he came back home, he decided to form a national airline. But others were moving rapidly to form their own airlines as well. One of the most famous of the competitors was Captain Eddie Rickenbacker of Columbus, whose own successful experiment would come to be called Eastern Airlines.

But Charles Lindbergh beat the competition to the gate. Working with Henry Ford of automobile fame, Lindbergh put together a company which would fly Ford Trimotor airplanes across the country. And if landing and transit rights couldn't be negotiated for everywhere the line would go, then the company would fly where it could and put people on trains where it couldn't.

In this way Transcontinental Air Transport (TAT) was born. On July 8, 1929, a group of people got off a train from New York at 7:35 AM and walked under a canopy across rain-swept parking lot to the brand new terminal of Port Columbus Airport. Port Columbus had been a dream of many people in Columbus for many years and was finally brought about after a bond issue passed in 1928.

After some speeches, the Lindberghs and other famous people like Amelia Earhart got on a plane called the City of Columbus and flew off into history. TAT was a shortlived experiment and it eventually merged into what came to be called Trans World Airlines. But Port Columbus was and continues to be a success. Over the years it has increased in size until it is many times larger than the original airport of 1929.

But the original terminal still stands at the southeast corner of the airport property, near the place where Fifth Avenue meets Hamilton Road. Special places are where the past and the future are constantly meeting each other. Port Columbus is one of those places.

Suffragettes at the Statehouse, c. 1914.
Courtesy of the Columbus Metropolitan Library.

~42~
Women's Suffrage

In 1920, the women of Ohio and the rest of the country finally got to do something free, white males in America had been doing for the previous few hundred years. They got the right to vote. It had been a long, hard struggle and Ohio in general and Columbus in particular had been right in the middle of it. For some reason, Ohio has been a hotbed of protest and agitation for equal rights for women for most of its history. Part of this is no doubt due to the fact that Ohio was one of the main cross roads of America in the 19th Century. In a time when few people lived west of the Mississippi, the old Northwest Territory was on the cutting edge of the frontier.

Many of the settlers of Ohio were either newly arrived immigrants from Europe or migrating residents of the east and south looking for a new start. And while these people brought much of their old culture with them, they were also more receptive than most people to the new ideas floating around their state.

It was a time when all sorts of new ideas and social movements were being born. Some were religious like the Mormons and the Shakers. Some were political like the death of Federalism and the rise of the new Whig, Greenback, and Nativist parties.

And some were social and cultural movements which would change the very fabric of American life. Among these were the temperance movement, which argued vigorously against the alcoholic fog which much of frontier America seemed quite happy to embrace. There was also the anti-slavery movement, which condemned to perdition any person of society that would presume to own other human beings. And then there were the women's rights advocates who argued that women should be as free and equal as men.

All of these movements had as many enemies as friends. Interestingly, many of the reformers who opposed slavery and alcohol also favored equal rights for women. The centers of agitation were often the campuses of America's colleges and universities. And since Ohio had more colleges per square mile than most places, it should not be too surprising to learn that the Buckeye State was a leader in the women's movement.

From places like Oberlin and Ohio Wesleyan came some of the first women college graduates in America. And from these beginnings, people like Lucy Stone and Elizabeth Cady Stanton forged a movement that sought equal rights for women in all aspects of American life.

As early as 1843, Abby Kelley Foster came to Columbus preaching anti-slavery and equality for women. Most of her male listeners were not amused. In 1861, Frances Dana Gage presented a petition to the Ohio Senate seeking the vote for women. It went nowhere. And over the course of the late 1800s, similar efforts to advance the cause of women's rights were not terribly successful.

By 1884, it was clear that a generalized approach to women's rights was not going to work. So more and more women began focusing their attention on one single issue and attaining victory for women by victory with that issue. That issue was THE VOTE.

Columbus had one of the strongest woman suffrage associations in the state and through the efforts of Elizabeth Coit, Rebecca Janney, Alice Peters and others, the battle was carried forth for the next two decades.

In 1909, women were being elected to the School Board in Columbus, but the right to vote in any and all elections was still to be won. The great confrontation over this issue came in 1912 when Ohio held a Constitutional Convention. Woman suffrage advocates organized marches, parades, and massive lobbying campaigns to win an election on this issue. An equally committed group of ladies worked just as hard to oppose the issue.

The campaign turned into one of the more lively confrontations in Columbus political history. The Anti-Suffrage Association adopted the motto, "the womanly woman does not want the vote." This immediately prompted a letter-writing campaign to the local press by several women who claimed they felt quite "womanly," thank you, and also wanted the right to vote. When the pro-suffrage campaign rented a floor in a downtown office building, the anti-suffrage activists rented the floor above them and made life interesting for the people working below.

On August 27, 1912, 5,000 women from across Ohio marched for woman suffrage in one of the more impressive parades ever seen in the capital city. After a long and hard-fought campaign, the issue went down to defeat by only 87,000 votes.

But even with this setback, the tide was seen to be turning. All across America, more and more women were winning the right to vote in local and state elections. It was only a matter of time before the vote would come.

It finally came in 1920 with the ratification of an amendment to the Constitution of the United States. With the passage of the amendment, the suffrage organizations either went out of business or transformed themselves into groups like the League of Women Voters, which continues to work to involve more people more directly in the political process.

Many people in the early 1920s thought the controversy, antagonisms, and arguments over women's rights would end once women got the vote. How wrong they were. The battles continue even unto the present day.

However the issues being debated are resolved, it is well to remember that vigorous disputation is a sign of a healthy republic. By that standard we are quite healthy indeed.

Gordon Battelle, c. 1929.
Courtesy of the Columbus Metropolitan Library.

~43~
Battelle Memorial Institute

Today the Battelle Memorial Institute is the largest private research organization in the world. With branches in Europe and America and thousands of employees in its farflung operations, Battelle is on the cutting edge of innovation in a number of fields of human endeavor. The company that refined and developed the xerox process is moving into the 21st Century with new initiatives which could and probably will have just as much impact on our world. How this all came to be, and the road Battelle took to get there, is one of the more interesting stories in the history of Columbus.

The story of Battelle began with steel and the men who made it. It is sometimes hard to believe, but modern steel making is really less than 150 years old. With the exception of expensive items like sword blades and special tools, steel was little used in the 19th Century. Iron was the metal of choice. Machines were made from iron. Bridges were built of iron. The fronting decoration called "iron lace" used on new and distinctively American buildings called was made of the material as well.

Then came the Bessemer process. Suddenly a new and cheap way to make high quality steel was available to anyone with the wit and the wherewithal to take advantage of it. And just as quickly a whole new group of men came forward to lead and direct the new industry.

They were a special breed of men. The task of making steel was, and still is, a rough, dirty, and dangerous business. The men who practiced steelmaking were physically strong, mentally sharp and as spiritually hardened as the metal they made. The men who managed them were stronger still. It took a special breed of individual to survive in this business.

It was said of Andrew Carnegie that he didn't know a thing about making steel—but he knew how to unrelentingly drive the men who did. Carnegie sold his steel business to J. P. Morgan in 1901 and spent the rest of his life giving libraries to cities and villages across America. Men like this were larger than life. Another such man was John Gordon Battelle.

And the place he finally made for himself was in the new and growing industry of steel making. He typified in his own way both the best and worst of late-19th Century capitalism. He was tough, honest and fair. And no one working with John Gordon Battelle worked harder than the man himself. He was also an assertive, unrelenting competitor who could make as many enemies as he made friends. In the course of his life, he made a great deal of money and spent precious little of it on himself. Most of it he set aside for his wife Annie and his child, Gordon. It was his hope that Gordon would carry on the work he had begun and be a better steelman than he ever was.

It was not to be. Gordon Battelle was many things that his father never was. He was well-mannered, well-educated, and well-liked. He also found it quite difficult to be the tough taskmaster that his father had been. His dream was not to use the family's wealth to perpetuate the family's role in the steel business, but to use it to benefit mankind.

When Gordon Battelle died in 1923, his wish began to come true. His will stipulated that the bulk of his rather sizeable estate be set aside to form a "Battelle Memorial Institute . . . for the encouragement of creative research . . . and the making of discoveries and inventions."

A board set up to develop and administer the Institute bought ten acres of land on King Avenue near the Olentangy River and set about the business of "creative research."

In its early years, the Institute largely reflected the goals and aspirations of its first Director—Dr. Horace W. Gillett. When he came to Battelle in 1929 to open the new facility, Gillett was one of the foremost researchers in America in the field of metallurgy and its applications. By the middle of the 1930s, Battelle had quickly become one of the world's pre-eminent centers for the study of metals in a scientific manner.

In 1934, Dr. Gillett asked the Board to appoint someone else as Director of the Institute so that he could spend more time on the research he did so well. The Board complied and hired a man named Clyde Williams.

Over the next 23 years, Williams reshaped Battelle into something unlike anything Dr. Gillett had tried to bring into being. Williams believed that the success of a private research organization like Battelle lay with being not only the best in one field but by being clearly superlative in many areas.

In the 1940s, Battelle became involved in the "Manhattan Project" and contributed significantly to the birth of the atomic age. At a later point, a frustrated inventor with a great idea but no capability to develop and market it came to Battelle for help. The Institute saw the value of the innovation and not only developed the process but retained ownership of some of it. The process was called "xerography" and the modern copier business is based on it.

By the time Clyde Williams resigned in 1957, the Institute had 3,100 employees worldwide and was spending over $25,000,000 per year. Over the next 20 years, the number of employees doubled and the budget of the Institute increased ten-fold. Battelle still is extending the limits of human knowledge in many different areas and is constantly seeking new ideas and innovations. For the sort of organization it is, Battelle is the biggest and best of its kind. Gordon Battelle would be pleased. And in his own way, perhaps his father would be pleased as well.

Statue of Elijah Pierce.
On Long Street, near the site of his barbershop.
Photo courtesy of Ed Lentz.

~44~
Elijah Pierce

Elijah Pierce was a man of many accomplishments. But he was not especially assertive about letting the world know about them. He spent most of his life as a barber and as a preacher of the Word of God as he understood it. But it was the way he preached that made him special.

He took the dreams and spirit and living heart of his religion and with the magic of his hands translated them into visions in wood. Elijah Pierce called himself a 'woodcarver,' but that description is about as understated as calling Michelangelo a 'ceiling painter.'

Elijah Pierce spent most of his life in Columbus. By the time he died here in 1984, he had created a sizeable body of work. But he had done more than that. He had also helped to reawaken public interest in a folk art form from an earlier era. Folk art in wood is alive and well in America, and some of the credit for keeping it that way is due to Elijah Pierce.

He was born on March 5, 1892, in a log cabin on a plantation in Baldwyn, Mississippi. He was the third of four children. His childhood was apparently happy enough and was at once centered around the cycles of seasonal work on the Prather Plantation and on the religious life of the black community in and around Baldwyn.

By the time he was eight, he was carving his name and simple designs into trees in the neighborhood. But with the encouragement of at least one uncle who was a woodcarver, he began to carve more elaborately. At a very early age, he realized he not only had an interest in woodcarving, he had a talent for doing it quite well indeed.

He also recognized that he was not happy living on a

farm in rural Mississippi. When he was eleven he began working for a local barber in Baldwyn. Combining his work at the barbershop with school proved to be a difficult task. Pierce finished the eighth grade and left school behind to work in Baldwyn and nearby Corinth, Mississippi, for the next several years.

After he turned 21, the pace of his life picked up.

In 1914, he joined the Mount Zion Baptist Church in Baldwyn and in the following year he married Zetta Palm. Zetta died after the birth of their first son, Willie, and Pierce's father died a few years later. The loss of these family members seemed to disorient the young man and he left Baldwyn for life on the road.

Living the life of an itinerant, Pierce worked at odd jobs and on construction crews, returning home from time to time to see his relatives. He would later say of this time that he "dressed well, danced well, and played the piano well."

He returned to Baldwyn long enough to be ordained in his home church and to receive a preacher's license in 1920. But soon he was on the road again. Like so many other people, black and white, he left the rural South after World War I to find his fortune in the North. In Danville, Illinois, he met Cornelia Houeston, who was originally from Columbus. When she returned to the capital city, he followed her and they were soon married. Until her death in 1948, the two were inseparable.

He took a job working as a barber in another man's shop until he opened his own shop in 1921. In the late 1920s, well-settled in Columbus, he began to carve again. Though his early work was general in theme, by the early '30s he was increasingly drawn to Biblical subjects. His most famous work from this period was the Book of Wood, which he finished in 1932. Illustrating the life of Christ and related religious themes, the Book of Wood's simple scenes are arranged across a series of wooden panels in bright colors.

Over the years, Elijah Pierce created hundreds of works of art in wood and gave away many of them to friends and acquaintances. In the 1930s and 1940s he and his wife travelled to fairs, exhibitions and religious meetings showing his work and explaining its meaning to the people in attendance.

Eventually he opened a gallery in his own barbershop on Long Street on the near east side of Columbus. To his customers and visitors to the shop, he would explain his way of working:

"And I usually pray over a piece of wood before I ever put a knife into it. I'm depending on Him for my inspiration and he give it to me. He said, 'Ask and you shall receive.'"

In the 1970s, Elijah Pierce came to be recognized as one of the premier living folk artists in America. His work was included in an increasing number of exhibitions and shows and he was becoming known in the national and international art circles.

By this time, Pierce had married Estelle Green and had taken on an aide and apprentice to help him with the work in the studio.

On May 7, 1984, Elijah Pierce died of a heart attack. The last piece he had been carving was a large crucifix made of a single piece of wood. He had been hoping to have it done by Easter, and he did. He died a few days later.

Today, a significant portion of the work of Elijah Pierce is represented in the permanent collections of the Columbus Museum of Art.

To Elijah Pierce this would not have been surprising. He always explained to people that his work was not done for himself but to express the faith and spirit that was such a central part of his life. As that faith lived on, so too would his work.

Emerson Burkhart, Self Portrait.
Courtesy of the Columbus Museum of Art.

45

Emerson Burkhart

He was an extremely talented American artist—certainly one of the best to ever live and work in Columbus. He was well-educated, well-traveled, and well-acquainted with the finer things in life. But he never lost the common touch acquired with his small town Ohio roots and was often at his best when he was teaching art rather than practicing it himself. He was also something of a iconoclast, an unabashed admirer of the female form, and one of the more opinionated people of his time. He was, in short, a rather complex fellow.

I never knew Emerson Burkhart. When he died in 1969, I was only aware of him by reputation. But local journalist Doral Chenoweth knew him well. He recorded several hours of tape with the artist and in 1970 wrote a play about him based on the tapes. Some of what follows is from that play.

Emerson Burkhart was born in Kalida, Ohio, on January 30, 1905. Putnam County in those days was in the rural heart of the Midwest and Burkhart grew up in a world that was not terribly complex. "Everything I remember was in black and white. My mother's dresses were white. Our house was white. My dad's suits were black. Everything else was in a dream world."

From an early age, he showed a talent for drawing. "I was branded the 'artist' from this time on to college days. Even some of my professors would call on the 'artist' to see what I had to say. When they needed a scroll drawn, a turkey, a pumpkin, stuff like that . . . I did it."

Like many American families, the Burkharts restlessly moved across America seeking new opportunities for a better life. While he was growing up, young Emerson lived in Texas, California, and Florida. But by the time he was a high school senior he was back in Kalida. His father wanted him to be a lawyer, but the young man wasn't sure what he wanted to do.

By way of compromise he enrolled in college as much to find himself as pursue a profession. The college was Ohio Wesleyan in Delaware, and Burkhart did well enough as a student. But eventually he was drawn to the art studio and school of Charles Hawthorne in Provincetown, Massachusetts.

"I didn't have much money so he let me sleep in the coal shed. . . . I painted it white on the inside . . . put in a bed and named it the 'black palace.' . . . I looked at him as the first real professional I had known."

Leaving Provincetown, Emerson Burkhart began a long journey in art that would take him some distance from the Kalida of his youth. It would not be a wealthy life, but then Emerson Burkhart was never greatly concerned about money.

"In my thinking, anybody who thinks in terms of money, doesn't know how to spend it. . . . I don't have a lot of money, but I sure know how to spend it. I have fun with what I have."

It was a good thing that he wasn't too concerned about money because there was not a great deal of it to go around in the early 1930s. The Great Depression had crippled America and many people scrambled on daily basis just to stay alive.

For a time, Burkhart sold hand-painted ties on the streets of Cincinnati and worked at various jobs—odd or otherwise. By 1931 he ended up in Columbus.

He joined the Artist's Project of the WPA, a government agency established to find work for the unemployed. Some of his work included a mural for the OSU School of Social Work and another mural for the wall above the stage in the auditorium of Central High School. Both murals still exist, but the Central High School one is not visible since zealous school officials put several coats of paint over it many years ago.

Over the years, Emerson Burkhart developed an abiding interest in two subjects—the female image and his own. He painted literally dozens of portraits of himself and of a variety of women in various poses. Along the way he maintained a running disputation with Columbus Art League about the nature of art in general and his in particular. Finally dissatisfied with the local artistic institutional community, he held annual showings of his work at his Woodland Avenue home for more than 30 years.

His partner in art was his wife Mary Ann. Of her, he said, "She never pushed me into making portraits, or commissions, or potboilers to make more money than we did. She would rather have a man paint a picture that was immortally a masterpiece. . . . This was the kind of idealism in her that I think is fabulous. She was the kind of woman I needed."

For many of those years, he accompanied artistic tours to various parts of the world, painting as he went. His work was exhibited in the Whitney Museum, the Carnegie Institute, the Art Institute of Chicago, and the Corcoran Gallery. Several pieces of his work reside in the Columbus Museum of Art as well.

As to the enduring value of his work, he once said, "Anyone who says he doesn't want to be famous is a liar. But I know I've done some really great paintings. I will just have to believe now that everything has its day and that my paintings will find their right place, in time."

The Grave Creek Mound in West Virginia, c. 1870.
No images of the Mound Street Mound exist, but it probably looked much like this one.
Courtesy of the Columbus Metropolitan Library.

46

The Mound on Mound Street

For thousands of years before the white man came, people had been living at the forks of the Scioto and Olentangy Rivers. The earliest people to live here were nomadic hunters about whom we know very little. They left little behind in their constant travels except an occasional arrowpoint.

But several hundred years ago, there emerged a more established series of civilizations of Native American peoples. These people stayed in one place, raised crops, and built quite permanent structures. The most permanent were a set of earthen mounds.

Some of the mounds were burial sites. Others were gathering places for ceremonial or religious purposes. Some of the great effigy mounds like Serpent Mound in Adams County probably served many purposes. It is clear and well-accepted that the people who built the mounds were Native Americans. As we learned more about these people, classifications came to be made based on the culture, lifestyle and evidence that they left behind.

Thus we know today that there was not one Moundbuilder culture but many. The names we have given these different cultures—Adena, Hopewell, Fort Ancient, and so on—refer to the places where evidence of their lives was first found. They are English names of American places and would make no sense to the people themselves, even if they were alive to hear them.

The reason these names were given to these ancient people is that we did not know what else to call them. Unlike the Sumerians, Egyptians, or the Maya, the Moundbuilders had no written language. And as far as we can tell, none of them left clear descendants from whom we could learn clues to the people themselves.

The Moundbuilders were gone by the time colonial settlers reached Ohio. Some theories propose that deadly wars, deadlier epidemics, and mergers with other tribes led to their disappearance. At this point we still really don't know. What we do know is that the key to understanding these people is the artifacts they left behind. Carefully preserving the sites and the cultural heritage of Ohio's first residents is something Ohio has been doing relatively well for the past century.

It wasn't always so. Columbus was laid out to be the new capital city of Ohio in 1812. A planned city, the town occupied the "High Banks opposite Franklinton at the Forks of the Scioto." One of the advantages of the site was that it was high, dry, and unoccupied.

But it had not always been unoccupied. As late as 1774, an Indian camp had been located near the Ohio Penitentiary. But evidence of even earlier residents was present as well. Joseph Sullivant, the son of the founder of Franklinton, claimed in later life that in the early days, there was a small mound in the center of the village of Franklinton, another near the Penitentiary, and two others on the other side of river near what is now Veterans Memorial. Every single one of these mounds was removed before any record was made of its location or contents.

While the removal of the small mounds is regrettable, what is harder to understand is the loss of the great mound in downtown Columbus.

When Joel Wright laid out Columbus, there was little to impede his placement of the rectangular grid of streets he proposed for the downtown. There was a creek or two and an occasional pond, but most of the land was flat and well-forested. And of course there was the mound. At the intersection of what is now Mound and High Streets was a 40-foot mound that was more than 300 feet around at its base. Towering above the river valley, it had a flat top more than 100 feet across.

Looking up at the mound, Joel Wright saw oak trees more than three feet in diameter growing out of the sides of the structure and five huge locust trees at the top. Wright decided to accept what he could not easily remove. He named the cross street Mound Street and diplomatically curved High Street around the Mound before heading it south once again.

An early settler, Dr. Young, bought the lot the mound sat on and built a two-story frame house at the top. He lived there for a time and was succeeded by a number other local families. Clay from the mound was used for a number of houses and for bricks for the original Statehouse at State and High Streets. But the mound itself still dominated the skyline as it had for generations. But after a number of years, the traffic on High Street began to increase as Columbus began to grow. And the great mound was seen to be less of a wonder and more of an impediment. So it was removed.

When the mound came down, all sorts of things were found. Some people discovered 'utensils.' Others found 'trinkets.' One man found a silver buckle that may have been a trade item from England or France. Another man found a skull so large it would fit over his own head. And bones were found as well. Many bones. Old bones. But most of them crumbled when exposed.

Some think a mound as high as that must have been used for signaling. There is another tall mound on McKinley Avenue and another near Worthington along the Olentangy. Perhaps there were others, now long gone as well. On clear nights these people may have carried torches to their mounds and spoken up and down the valley one to another. It is part of the lingering yearning of our common humanity with the people who preceded us that causes us to ask—who did they signal and what did they say?

~Further Reading~

At the end of the first *As It Were*, I listed a few books I found useful about the history of Columbus and which I used with some frequency.

I am repeating the list because these books are still the best place to start when seeking further information on the history of this part of the world. The best places to find them are in the History, Biography and Travel Division at the Main Branch of the Columbus Metropolitan Library, The Archives Library of the Ohio Historical Society at The Ohio Historical Center, and the State Library of Ohio in downtown Columbus. Most local university libraries also have many of these books.

Garrett, Betty, *Columbus, America's Crossroads*, 1980.

Hooper, Osman C., *History of Columbus, Ohio*, 1920.

Lee. Alfred E., *History of Columbus*, 2 vols., 1892.

Martin, William T., *History of Franklin County*, 1858.

Moore, Opha, *History of Franklin County, Ohio,* 3 vols, 1930.

Studer, Jacob, *History of Columbus, Ohio*, 1872.